Cambridge Elements

Elements in Gender and Politics
edited by
Tiffany D. Barnes
University of Texas at Austin
Diana Z. O'Brien
Washington University in St. Louis

ABORTION ATTITUDES AND POLARIZATION IN THE AMERICAN ELECTORATE

Erin C. Cassese
University of Delaware
Heather L. Ondercin
Appalachian State University
Jordan Randall
Appalachian State University

Shaftesbury Road, Cambridge CB2 8EA, United Kingdom

One Liberty Plaza, 20th Floor, New York, NY 10006, USA

477 Williamstown Road, Port Melbourne, VIC 3207, Australia

314–321, 3rd Floor, Plot 3, Splendor Forum, Jasola District Centre, New Delhi – 110025, India

103 Penang Road, #05–06/07, Visioncrest Commercial, Singapore 238467

Cambridge University Press is part of Cambridge University Press & Assessment, a department of the University of Cambridge.

We share the University's mission to contribute to society through the pursuit of education, learning and research at the highest international levels of excellence.

www.cambridge.org
Information on this title: www.cambridge.org/9781009533133

DOI: 10.1017/9781009533119

© Erin C. Cassese, Heather L. Ondercin, and Jordan Randall 2025

This publication is in copyright. Subject to statutory exception and to the provisions of relevant collective licensing agreements no reproduction of any part may take place without the written permission of Cambridge University Press & Assessment.

When citing this work, please include a reference to the DOI 10.1017/9781009533119

First published 2025

A catalogue record for this publication is available from the British Library

ISBN 978-1-009-53313-3 Hardback
ISBN 978-1-009-53315-7 Paperback
ISSN 2753-8117 (online)
ISSN 2753-8109 (print)

Additional resources for this publication at www.cambridge.org/abortionattitudes

Cambridge University Press & Assessment has no responsibility for the persistence or accuracy of URLs for external or third-party internet websites referred to in this publication and does not guarantee that any content on such websites is, or will remain, accurate or appropriate.

Abortion Attitudes and Polarization in the American Electorate

Elements in Gender and Politics

DOI: 10.1017/9781009533119
First published online: January 2025

Erin C. Cassese
University of Delaware

Heather L. Ondercin
Appalachian State University

Jordan Randall
Appalachian State University

Author for correspondence: Erin C. Cassese, ecassese@udel.edu

Abstract: About two-thirds of Americans support legal abortion in many or all circumstances, and this group finds itself a frustrated majority following the Supreme Court's 2022 decision in *Dobbs v. Jackson Women's Health Organization* which overturned the legal precedent set in *Roe v. Wade*. Previous scholarship argues intense minorities can secure favorable policy outcomes when facing off against a more diffuse and less motivated majority, creating incongruence between public opinion and policy. This Element focuses on the ways that preference intensity and partisan polarization have contributed to the current policy landscape surrounding abortion rights. Using survey data from the American National Election Studies, the authors identify Americans with intense preferences about abortion and investigate the role they play in electoral politics. They observe a shift in the relationship between partisanship and preference intensity coinciding with *Dobbs* and speculate about what this means for elections and policy congruence in the future.

Keywords: public opinion, polarization, abortion, reproductive rights, affect, voter mobilization, campaigns and elections

© Erin C. Cassese, Heather L. Ondercin, and Jordan Randall 2025

ISBNs: 9781009533133 (HB), 9781009533157 (PB), 9781009533119 (OC)
ISSNs: 2753-8117 (online), 2753-8109 (print)

Contents

1 Frustrated Majorities, Intense Minorities, and Abortion Policy — 1

2 A Brief History of Abortion Rights in America — 7

3 State Variation in Abortion Policy Post-*Dobbs* — 25

4 Abortion Attitudes and Partisanship in the American Electorate — 35

5 Preference Intensity and Abortion-Focused Americans — 44

6 Abortion Focus and Polarization — 56

7 Electoral Politics Post-*Dobbs* — 70

References — 87

An online appendix for this publication can be accessed at www.cambridge.org/abortionattitudes

1 Frustrated Majorities, Intense Minorities, and Abortion Policy

In early May of 2022, *Politico* published a leaked draft of the Supreme Court's decision in *Dobbs v. Jackson Women's Health Organization* indicating that the Court intended to overturn constitutional protections for abortion established in the 1973 *Roe v. Wade* decision. Upon release of the official opinion the following month, the policy landscape changed dramatically across the country, as states were permitted to adopt a wider range of policies. Abortion was immediately banned in thirteen states as trigger laws went into effect (Nash and Guarnieri 2022). Other states quickly took steps to adopt more restrictive policies that narrowed the timeframe during which abortion was permissible; eliminated exceptions to abortion restrictions related to rape, incest, maternal health, and fetal abnormalities; and even criminalized abortion and the provision of assistance to anyone seeking one. Alternatively, a small number of states moved to better secure abortion rights.

Dobbs clearly sent a shock wave through the United States, representing a major victory for the anti-abortion movement with dramatic repercussions for the rights of pregnant people. But, as *shocking* as this decision appeared to be for the American public, it's worth asking whether *Dobbs* was, in fact, *surprising*. After all, well-funded, high-profile anti-abortion groups had worked to overturn *Roe* for decades, finding success through wide-ranging strategies at the state and federal levels involving candidate recruitment, lobbying, legislation, regulatory action, direct ballot measures, legal challenges, and influencing court appointments, as well as direct action campaigns organized by activists (Luker 1984; Ziegler 2020). Likewise, leaders in the Republican Party had openly called for *Roe* to be overturned, and they had finally installed a conservative majority on the Supreme Court. The justices in this majority had been explicitly vetted for their opposition to abortion rights (Green 2022). Feminists and other reproductive justice activists, meanwhile, had been warning of this very outcome, becoming increasingly vocal on the issue following Donald Trump's victory in 2016.

For many, the *Dobbs* decision was a shock *and* a surprise, in large part because a majority of Americans consistently opposed this outcome. In a Gallup survey conducted immediately following the *Dobbs* leak, 63 percent of Americans disagreed with the Court's decision to overturn *Roe*.[1] Public opinion was actually aligned fairly well with the guidelines set out in *Roe,* which legalized abortion within certain limits. During a pregnant woman's

---
[1] These data are from a Gallup survey conducted May 2–22, 2022 (Abortion 2024).

first trimester, she and her doctor had discretion over whether to terminate her pregnancy.[2] In the second trimester, states were permitted to regulate abortion except when a pregnant woman's life was at stake.[3] Majority opinion was well represented by this conditional framework. In the same 2022 Gallup survey, 50 percent of Americans agreed that abortion should be legal in some circumstances. Another 35 percent felt abortion should be legal under any circumstances, and only a minority, 13 percent, felt abortion should be illegal in all circumstances. Disaggregating opinion to the state level is similarly instructive. According to a recent report from the Public Religion Research Institute (PRRI), a majority of Americans believe that abortion should be legal in all or most cases in forty-five of fifty states. There is no state in which more than 16 percent of Americans believe abortion should be completely banned (PRRI 2024), meaning many of the state laws banning or severely restricting abortion that went into effect because of *Dobbs* align with the views of only a small minority of Americans.[4]

The cascade of changes stemming from the *Dobbs* decision pushed policy further away from the preferences of the American public and produced what public opinion scholars refer to as a "frustrated majority" (Hill 2022). Frustrated majorities occur when public support for a policy is not reflected in the law. In fact, frustrated majorities are fairly common in American politics (Lax and Phillips 2012). While common, they are concerning, because in democratic political systems, there is a normative expectation that policy should reflect the will of its citizens. Frustrated majorities therefore raise critical questions about whether our democracy is working as intended and the quality of representation Americans receive from elected officials.[5]

How did we arrive at a position where policy and opinion on abortion are incongruent? The answer to this question is complex. Policy pertaining to abortion rights involves myriad political actors and organizations working across institutions and levels of government. Over time, opponents of abortion operating at the intersection of religious organizations, social movements, and

---

[2] Historically, policies governing reproductive rights use the terms "women" and "mother," and this language is also used in the survey questions analyzed below. We continue to use these terms in this Element despite their narrowness, but recognize these policies refer to the rights of all people who can become pregnant, including non-binary people and trans men.

[3] The Supreme Court moved away from the trimester framework in their 1983 decision *City of Akron v. Akron Center for Reproductive Health*. See Section 2 for further discussion of the evolution of abortion policy and the courts' decisions.

[4] Disaggregating from national samples to obtain state-level estimates, even with large samples, requires caution (Caughey and Warshaw 2022). More on this to come in Section 3.

[5] Scholars disagree as to whether frustrated majorities always reflect anti-democratic outcomes. Majoritarian outcomes can yield normatively undesirable results, for instance, when majorities suppress the basic rights of minorities. For competing perspectives, see Hill (2022) and Levitsky and Ziblatt (2023).

organized interest groups worked successfully on a variety of these fronts to limit the exercise of abortion rights before securing the Supreme Court justices who delivered the *Dobbs* decision (e.g., Bentele et al. 2018; Haugeberg 2017; Kreitzer 2015). But electoral politics have played an important role in policy change as well. Campaign promises about abortion rights have featured prominently in efforts to mobilize Americans, particularly Americans with intense, deeply held preferences on the issue (Bonilla 2022).[6]

While considerable scholarly attention has emphasized the role of formally organized interest groups in shaping abortion policy (e.g., Carmines et al. 2010), in this Element we focus on Americans with intense preferences about abortion in order to better understand an important and ongoing influence on abortion rights policy and American elections. These Americans are informally united by their intense preferences and exert significant political influence. Drawing on intensity theory (Hill 2022), we make a case for why preference intensity is critical for understanding the interplay between elections, policy, and representation, particularly in the case of abortion rights. Existing work on abortion attitudes has found evidence that policy responds to public opinion, but this work has focused exclusively on state policymaking under *Roe* and, until very recently, the federal standard set by *Roe* constrained the potential scope of responsiveness. In addition, this past work has largely overlooked the role of preference intensity in driving representation on abortion rights. Our contribution is to integrate these factors to gain a richer understanding of opinion-policy congruence in the period leading up to and immediately following the *Dobbs* decision, which marked a historic shift in the policy space.

Preference Intensity and a Frustrated Majority on Abortion Rights

Winning elections is fundamentally a mobilization game, and office seekers must maximize their vote share to gain office. One school of thought – the folk theory of democracy – suggests candidates should accomplish this by locating and appealing to a "median voter" who represents the positions held by the majority of the electorate (Achen and Bartels 2017; Downs 1957; Feddersen et al. 1990). Unsurprisingly, this approach is expected to produce an outcome where an office seeker maximizes their vote share and the preferences of the majority are reflected in policy – in other words, a majoritarian outcome. But the way policy preferences are distributed in the electorate is only part of the story. Not only do people hold different positions on an issue, they also hold these positions with different degrees

---

[6] These folks go by many names in the political science literature: single-issue voters, issue publics, and sometimes policy demanders (Bawn et al. 2012; Ryan and Ehlinger 2023).

of intensity. It turns out that preference intensity is critical because it changes the strategic calculus for elites and office seekers.

Intense minorities can be very effective at drawing elite support to their causes. This is a key insight from Seth Hill's (2022) work on frustrated majorities. Hill argues that citizens with intense preferences are more engaged in politics and dedicate more resources to pursuing representation. Their investment in political action sends a signal to office seekers about their commitment to an issue and their intention to engage further in pursuit of their goal (see also Bishin 2009). Because preference intensity is so tightly tied to political behavior, office seekers may secure more electoral gain from appealing to an intense minority compared to a more diffuse, less engaged majority represented by the median voter (e.g., Achen and Bartels 2017; Bishin 2009). They make promises to an intense minority (e.g., committing to nominate conservative Supreme Court justices) in exchange for reliable electoral support (Bonilla 2022). Through this pathway, intense minorities can exert a disproportionate influence on policy. This is one of several mechanisms that have influenced the current state of policy on abortion rights at both the state and federal levels.

Parties are an important piece of the puzzle here too. Over time, the Democratic and Republican parties have staked out increasingly distinct positions on abortion rights. In the years that followed the *Roe* decision, the Democratic Party became more supportive of abortion rights whereas the Republican Party grew increasingly opposed to them. In other words, the parties have become more polarized in their positions on abortion rights. When political polarization is high, as it is at present, a median voter strategy becomes less useful and it becomes easier for parties to side with an intense minority (Dyck and Pearson-Merkowitz 2023; Levitsky and Ziblatt 2023; Svolik 2019). Politicians know they are unlikely to lose votes to the other party due to the distance between them and other factors, like negative partisanship. The key is to turn out their base. If the party base includes a minority of sufficient size and intensity, targeted appeals to this group may produce greater electoral returns than an approach aimed at the majority position (Hill 2022).

In the pages that follow, we take a close look at Americans with intense preferences about abortion.[7] We are interested not only in the positions Americans take (i.e., whether they support or oppose abortion rights), but the intensity with which they hold their positions.[8] Using data from the American

---

[7] Hill's (2022) conceptualization of intensity theory and the role preference intensity plays in creating frustrated majorities is not specific to any single issue. Hill presents case studies of policymaking efforts around stem cell research and gun control in his book on this topic.

[8] In this Element, we use the terms "supporters of abortion rights" and "opponents of abortion" rather than alternatives like "pro-choice"/"pro-life" because the survey does not include direct measures of self-identification with the pro-choice/pro-life labels. Research also suggests that the public sometimes uses the labels in unexpected ways or eschews them all together (e.g., LaRoche et al. 2024).

National Election Studies, we derive a measure of preference intensity for abortion policy and use it to identify the "abortion-focused Americans" who likely represent an intense minority on abortion rights. Our approach suggests these abortion-focused Americans sit on both sides of the political aisle. Regardless of their partisan orientation, they are distinct from Americans with less-intense abortion preferences in a few important ways. Namely, they hold more extreme positions when it comes to abortion policy, they have more intense emotional reactions to political parties, candidates, and issues, *and* they participate in politics at higher rates than Americans with less intense preferences.

Although there are abortion-focused Americans in both parties, their efforts to influence policy do not cancel one another out. Abortion-focused Americans are not equally represented in both parties; the Republican Party has historically contained a more sizable intense minority. The partisan asymmetry we uncover helps to explain an important contributing factor to why policy has drifted against abortion rights even when a majority of Americans now support them – members of this group have disproportionately communicated extreme anti-abortion positions to elected officials and office seekers.

Broader aspects of the party and electoral systems may have encouraged the Republican Party to be particularly responsive to this intense minority of abortion-focused Americans. The New Deal realignment in the 1930s meant the Republican Party faced a numerical minority for decades.[9] As the smaller of the two major parties, Republicans were incentivized to find ways to assemble and maintain a coalition of voters to win elections. The New Deal coalition weakened during the 1960s and 1970s, when the electoral bases of the parties shifted in response to major legislation like the 1964 Civil Rights Act and the *Roe* decision. Evangelical Protestants, newly mobilized by the *Roe* decision, became central to the Republican Party's electoral coalition.[10]

As we show in a coming section, evangelicals and people who attend church frequently are more likely than other Americans to have intense preferences about abortion rights. Our findings are consistent with the theory that office seekers will appeal to intense minorities in exchange for electoral support, and this historical numeric disadvantage may have created more incentive to do so for the Republican Party.[11] During the last several decades, this electoral strategy has proven successful for the Republican Party, and Republicans have leveraged this

---

[9] In the past ten years, the Republican Party and Democratic Party have essentially reached parity in the electorate, largely as a result of the increasing number of independent identifiers (Pew Research Center 2024).

[10] Among other political developments, notably desegregation (Balmer 2021).

[11] Differences in the party organizations and cultures also contributed to the increased influence of abortion-focused voters within the Republican Party relative to the Democratic Party. The Republican Party is more homogeneous, in both demographic and ideological terms

success, along with efforts on other fronts, to shape abortion policy in the United States and frustrate majority preferences on abortion rights.

Dobbs may have changed the electoral calculus when it comes to abortion rights once again. Many of the media narratives surrounding the 2022 midterms elections focused on mobilization among a frustrated majority of Americans who supported the *Roe* standard. For example, voter registration data pointed to an increase in registration rates among women, particularly in states with direct ballot measures (Paris and Cohn 2022). And survey data suggest abortion was a critical issue priority among Democratic voters (KFF 2022; Pew Research Center 2022). There are also some signs that the Republican Party felt more constrained in its ability to cater to its intense minority of abortion-focused partisans than in the past. In September of 2022, Senator Lindsey Graham (R-SC) introduced a 15-week federal abortion ban. Rather than capitalize on the momentum of the *Dobbs* decision, other office-seeking Republicans, including former president Trump, backed away from Graham's position, despite this kind of ban featuring prominently in the party platform for decades. After investigating the relationship preference intensity, mobilization, and representation prior to *Dobbs*, we turn our attention to how this framework can help us to understand how these dynamics are likely to shape elections and efforts to shift policy in the post-*Dobbs* era.

Plan of This Element

Our goals in this Element are to provide the historical context necessary for understanding the current policy landscape surrounding abortion rights and to demonstrate, using public opinion data, how an intense minority succeeded in frustrating the representation of a majority of Americans on abortion rights. Abortion politics in the United States has a long and complex history, and the next three sections are dedicated to providing important historical perspective. Section 2 includes a brief overview of abortion politics in the United States leading up to the *Roe* decision, and a more detailed look at the role of the courts in shaping policy between the *Roe* and *Dobbs* decisions. In this section, we highlight the correspondence between abortion policy and public opinion and discuss the role abortion has played in electoral politics. Section 3 examines policy change stemming from the *Dobbs* decision, which removed constitutional protection for abortion and provided greater freedom for states to set abortion policy. While some states chose to expand abortion rights, many states moved against public opinion to restrict abortion rights. In Section 4, we report

---

(Grossman and Hopkins 2016; Noel 2014). Abortion-focused Americans had to vie for power with other intense minorities within a much more heterogeneous Democratic Party.

trends in public attitudes toward abortion policy and explain how the parties became more distinct in their positions on this issue over time.

In the remaining sections, we turn to preference intensity and its role in electoral politics. In Section 5, we discuss the challenges associated with measuring preference intensity, then outline our own approach, which relies on mentions of abortion in open-ended party evaluation questions asked in the American National Election Studies. We report the political and demographic factors associated with intense abortion preferences, drawing out comparisons between "abortion-focused" Americans and those with less intense preferences. Section 6 explores the relationship between preference intensity and polarization in the American electorate. We find that abortion-focused Americans are more polarized than people with weaker preferences in several respects – they participate in politics at higher rates, report stronger emotional reactions to politics, and hold not only more intense preferences, but also more extreme preferences. This set of findings is consistent with the signaling mechanism described in intensity theory – people with intense preferences engage in more frequent and costly forms of political behavior, signaling their commitment to political elites and securing a commitment to represent them in return. This process can result in an intense minority outmaneuvering a more diffuse majority.

The concluding section evaluates the impact of preference intensity on electoral behavior in the immediate aftermath of the *Dobbs* decision – a time when, as we demonstrate using analysis of the *New York Times* and *Wall Street Journal*, abortion salience was at a record high. Using data from the 2022 ANES pilot study, we create a proxy for abortion focus and compare the prevalence, attitudes, and behavior of abortion-focused Americans across party lines. We conclude by speculating about what our findings mean for the future of policy and its relationship to public opinion, given the continued salience of abortion and the changing electoral calculus facing both parties when it comes to representing constituent preferences on abortion rights.

2 A Brief History of Abortion Rights in America

Norma McCorvey became pregnant for a third time in 1969 while living in Texas (Prager 2013).[12] Having lost custody of her first child and given a second child up for adoption, McCorvey wanted to end her pregnancy. However,

---

[12] Norma's McCorvey's story is complicated. There have been inconsistencies in her recounting of her life experiences, her extent of participation in the *Roe v. Wade* case, and her personal position on abortion rights over time (Prager 2013; Solly 2022). Notably, McCorvey became vocally opposed to abortion later in life, only to later claim that pro-life groups had paid her to make this public conversion (Serjeant 2020).

Texas's strict abortion law only allowed a pregnancy to be terminated in cases where carrying a fetus to full term endangered the life of the mother. McCorvey lacked the resources to travel out of state to a location where elective abortion was legal. Eventually, she was referred to Sarah Weddington and Linda Coffee, lawyers looking for a client to challenge Texas's abortion law. Weddington and Coffee filed a suit in federal court on behalf of Norma McCorvey under the pseudonym Jane Roe. The lawsuit alleged that Texas's abortion statute was too vague and violated the protections for individual liberty established by the Ninth and Fourteenth Amendments (Solly 2022). McCorvey was never able to get the abortion she wanted; she gave birth before the federal district court ruled in her favor. The case made its way to the Supreme Court, and several years afterward, in 1973, the *Roe v. Wade* ruling established a constitutional right to an abortion.

The fractured nature of the US political system means that abortion policy is set at both national and state levels and across the legislative, executive, and judicial branches of government, resulting in a complex policy space. The case of *Roe v. Wade* illustrates just a little bit of this complexity by highlighting how state legislatures can be constrained by federal courts. When the Court issued its ruling, it not only invalidated Texas's law but also similar laws in forty-four other states. The *Roe* decision allowed states to regulate abortion after the first trimester of pregnancy, and the years that followed its passage were marked by new legislation and subsequent challenges in various state and federal courts. As a consequence, abortion policy was fragmented, even with the constitutional protection afforded by *Roe* in place. Now that *Dobbs* has eliminated this federal standard and returned the authority to set abortion policy to the states, abortion policy has become even more complex and variable nationwide.

In this section, we offer a brief history of abortion policy in the United States to provide context for the *Dobbs* decision and the creation of a frustrated majority of supporters of abortion rights in the United States. We start with a look at major developments in abortion policy prior to *Roe* to illustrate the long history of efforts to regulate abortion that preceded the Supreme Court's decision. *Roe* marked an important shift in the use of the federal courts to set policy in this area, and we review the mechanisms intense minorities can use to leverage the courts in pursuit of their policy aims. This information is useful for understanding the trajectory of court decisions and public policy between *Roe* and *Dobbs*. Though the shift in precedent may have seemed sudden, especially to members of the public who were previously not paying much attention to state-level policy developments in this area, *Dobbs* was preceded by a series of court decisions that incrementally drew policy further out of alignment with public opinion. A focus on the federal courts and intense minorities during this period provides critical insight into how abortion policy has become misaligned with public opinion over time.

Abortion Policy Prior to the *Roe v. Wade* Decision

In the majority opinion for *Dobbs*, Justice Alito argued that the legal basis for *Roe*, which based the right to an abortion on the protections afforded in the Due Process Clause of the Fourteenth Amendment, was invalid because rights deriving from this constitutional basis must be "deeply rooted in this Nation's history and tradition" and "implicit in the concept of ordered liberty." Abortion, Alito contended, "does not fall within this category." Several parties have taken issue with this rationale, especially with its characterization of the history of abortion in the United States (American Historical Association 2022; Center for Reproductive Rights 2023a). Reproductive politics, and abortion rights in particular, have a complicated history in the United States. In this Element, we provide some context for the contemporary debate over the historical significance of abortion sparked by the *Dobbs* decision.

Women have long used abortion as a means to manage their fertility and health, regardless of whether they were afforded a legal right to the procedure. Historically, factors like race, class, and geographic location have shaped women's legal bodily autonomy, including abortion rights (Solinger 2019). Abortion policymaking efforts are deeply entwined with debates involving women's rights, scientific authority, and religious belief (Solinger 2019; Spruill 2017; Ziegler 2020), meaning debates over abortion rights have historically been contentious and involved the competing interests of multiple parties. The policy that emerged from these debates influenced every aspect of the exercise of abortion rights – where abortion could take place, who performed the procedure, how the procedure was performed, who could access abortion services, and how abortion was financed.

Early abortion policy in the United States was heavily influenced by the "born alive" rule derived from English Common Law. This rule maintained that a fetus was not entitled to the same rights as a living person, and that abortion was not viewed as murder (Rose 2007). Although a fetus was conferred some legal rights, those rights were not fully realized until birth. Abortion was largely viewed as permissible until quickening, when a woman could feel her fetus move, typically at some point in the second trimester of pregnancy. Without accurate means to determine if a woman was pregnant and whether a pregnancy had reached the quickening stage, early abortions were often deemed legal or ignored (Ziegler 2020). A different set of laws governed the reproductive capacity of enslaved women during this period. After the slave trade was outlawed in 1808, the reproductive potential of enslaved women became a priority for slaveholders, and they sometimes resorted to abortion as an act of resistance (Solinger 2019).

Starting in the mid-1800s, the first organized anti-abortion movement emerged in the United States, largely led by the newly professionalized medical establishment. During this period, the practice of medicine was carried out by a combination of "regular doctors" who were formally trained in medical schools, and laypeople, such as midwives, who had obtained their knowledge and skills in less formal settings. Abortions were fairly common, with estimates ranging from 20 percent to 30 percent of pregnancies ending in abortion (Luker 1984; Solinger 2019). Although there is no public opinion data to draw on from this period, the information we do have about abortion rates suggests that the procedure was acceptable to a fair amount of the public and widely considered part of women's regular reproductive health care (Luker 1984).

Gradually, licensed medical professionals used the issue of abortion as a means to elevate themselves over lay practitioners, like midwives (Mohr 1978). The burgeoning medical establishment argued for restricting abortion on the grounds that women lacked the medical expertise necessary to decide whether to end their pregnancies (Luker 1984). They also worked to shift the framing away from the common law understanding of abortion to characterize abortion as the murder of an unborn child (Luker 1984). Laws passed at the turn of the century enhanced the authority of doctors, who were largely men, to determine whether abortion was medically necessary. Federal legislation aimed at regulating obscene materials, notably the Comstock Act of 1873, further restricted the distribution of information about how to terminate a pregnancy along with the devices used to prevent or terminate pregnancy by criminalizing the use of the postal service for these purposes (Luthra 2024). This law helped to solidify the medical establishment's control over the provision of abortion services.

The medical establishment also advanced a eugenic rationale for limiting women's reproduction (Solinger 2019). In the mid-to-late 1800s, a large influx of immigrants, mainly from eastern and southern Europe, shifted the ethnic and religious composition of the United States. At the same time, large swaths of the population were shifting from rural areas into urban centers, and the economy was transitioning from an agricultural to industrial focus. Under these conditions, birth rates among the white population declined. Many medical professionals viewed the newer immigrant groups as genetically inferior and worried that high birth rates among immigrants relative to whites would have disastrous implications for the future of the United States. To address this concern, they sought to restrict access to birth control and abortion for white women in order to counteract declining birth rates.

By 1910, state-level abortion bans were widespread, but states did not consistently enforce these laws and primarily relied on doctors' authority to determine when the procedure was medically necessary. By the 1940s and 1950s, states started to more consistently pursue abortion providers and the women who sought abortions (Solinger 2019). As doctors and medical facilities became increasingly concerned about being targeted by law enforcement, hospitals established review boards to assess whether abortions were medically necessary on a case-by-case basis. These medical boards had considerable discretion in determining what counted as medically necessary, and they often did not include the patient's personal physician, limiting the influence of the doctor who was most familiar with the case (Rose 2007).

The targeting of abortion providers and other legal restrictions did not put an end to abortion. Instead, it limited women's access to *safe* abortion. Absent other options, many women attempted to self-abort or sought abortions from providers without appropriate training, risking their health and long-term fertility. Women of lower socioeconomic status and racial minorities were particularly vulnerable to negative health outcomes resulting from efforts to terminate pregnancies at this time (Solinger 2019).

Two events in the 1950s and 1960s focused the American public's attention on the potential pitfalls of current abortion law (Rosenberg 2008). First, there was a rubella outbreak in California. Rubella, also known as German measles, can cause serious birth defects, especially if a woman is infected in the first three months of pregnancy. California state law would not allow for abortion under these circumstances, leaving many doctors frustrated by the constraints on their standard of care (Luker 1984). According to the Centers for Disease Control, between 1964 and 1965, 12.5 million cases of rubella occurred in the United States, resulting in 11,000 miscarriages, 2,100 infant deaths, and 20,000 babies born with congenital rubella syndrome (Rubella 2020).[13]

Second, the drug thalidomide, used to treat nausea during pregnancy, was linked to serious birth defects (Rose 2007). Thalidomide was initially available over the counter in many European countries, and then removed from the market in 1961 after its connections to poor fetal health outcomes became clear. Sherri Finkbine, mother of four and producer and host of a popular children's TV show, sought to obtain an abortion after using thalidomide to help with morning sickness (Solinger 2019). When the review board at Finkbine's local hospital

---

[13] Congenital rubella syndrome occurs when a mother contracts Rubella in the first twelve weeks of pregnancy and can lead to miscarriage, still birth, and severe birth defects. Thanks to a vaccine developed in 1969, rubella is currently quite rare in the United States. The CDC recommends that all children receive the MMR vaccine, which protects against measles, mumps, and rubella. Additionally, the CDC recommends that women who are planning to get pregnant ensure they are vaccinated at least four weeks before becoming pregnant. For more information see: www.cdc.gov/rubella/index.html.

denied her request for an abortion, she traveled to Sweden. The Swedish obstetrician performing the abortion examined the fetus and noted abnormalities that were incompatible with life (Luker 1984). Finkbine's story received extensive media coverage and sparked intense public debate, ultimately raising awareness about women's limited reproductive options in the United States.

Recognizing the public health crises arising from legal prohibitions on abortion, some medical professionals and women's health advocates mobilized to promote decriminalization (Luker 1984; Solinger 2019). They argued that providing doctors with greater control over women's access to reproductive options including abortion would lead to improved health outcomes. In 1959, the American Law Institute (ALI) proposed model legislation to legalize abortions in cases of rape, incest, severe fetal abnormality, or a threat to women's health (Lewis 1959). Before 1972, about one third of states adopted legal reforms based on the ALI model (Shimabukuro 2009). While the medical community largely led these reform efforts, the growing feminist movement also advocated for more expansive reproductive rights, arguing that the new laws did little to increase access to abortion services and more substantial legal changes were needed for women to exercise a fuller range of reproductive choices (Ziegler 2020).

Public reaction to these critical events suggests that laws restricting or even criminalizing abortion were out of line with public opinion at the time. In a 1962 Gallup poll, 52 percent of respondents supported Sherri Finkbine's decision to seek an abortion, while 32 percent opposed it (Brenan 2018). A series of Gallup Surveys conducted in the 1960s demonstrate that a clear majority of Americans supported legalized abortion in situations when the woman or fetus faced a significant health risk. Higher levels of disapproval were expressed for more elective circumstances, such as not wanting to have more children and for financial reasons (Blake 1971). Though multiple states had started to liberalize their abortion laws in the decade before *Roe v. Wade*, abortion policy was largely out of step with public attitudes toward abortion rights.

Over time, efforts by abortion rights activists chipped away at state-level abortion bans, securing greater legal access to abortion in seventeen states by 1973. When efforts in the state legislatures to reform abortion laws stalled, the feminist movement turned to the courts to protect women's reproductive rights (Rosenberg 2008). The civil rights movement had success in leveraging the courts to enact change, and the feminist movement hoped they could achieve similar success by pressing the courts to establish a constitutional basis for reproductive rights. Because this period reflects an important shift in the use of the federal courts to set abortion policy, we review the mechanisms intense minorities can use to influence the courts and secure representation. Over time, intense minorities on both sides of the debate over abortion rights have effectively leveraged the court to pursue their policy goals. These efforts have sometimes contributed to policy outcomes that frustrated majority opinion.

Intensity Theory, the Courts, and Abortion Rights

Abortion politics presents multiple paths for minority influence. Intensity theory argues that frustrated majorities arise when public officials, primarily legislators, respond to an intense minority engaging in costly political action because they expect it will boost their likelihood of electoral success (Hill 2022). This account of minority influence often overlooks the ways that other political institutions can be leveraged to accomplish their objectives, including institutions populated by appointed rather than elected officials. We argue the history of policymaking surrounding abortion highlights the ways the courts can contribute to the formation of frustrated majorities.

Lifetime appointments to the federal bench were intended to free the judiciary from the electoral pressures facing the legislative and executive branches of government. However, the lack of an electoral connection does not completely isolate the courts. Instead, public opinion can influence the courts both directly and indirectly. Direct influence means the court takes public opinion into account when making its rulings. Before the start of the Burger Court in 1969, there was a correlation between public opinion and Supreme Court decision-making, suggesting this direct pathway was at work (Johnson and Strother 2021). However, correlations between opinion and decision-making are not found after 1960, when the Court made its key rulings on abortion. Thus, influence likely occurs only through indirect means.

In an indirect pathway of influence, the public elects officials who appoint judges. The expectation is that judicial decision-making will reflect public opinion broadly or, at least, the preferences of the elected officials' constituents. Office seekers often work to forge this connection in the minds of voters through campaign promises to appoint sympathetic justices to the Supreme Court or the federal bench.[14] Some legal scholars also consider the courts indirectly constrained by public opinion because courts lack the power and resources to enforce their decisions (Hall 2014; Rosenberg 2008; VanSickle-Ward and Hollis-Brusky 2013). As a result, federal courts rely on elected officials in the executive and legislative branches of government for implementation. They must consider

---

[14] For example, the Republican Party platform has promised to appoint conservative Supreme Court justices every year since 1996. Alternatively, the 1984 Democratic Party platform mentions that Reagan's SCOTUS appointments had stripped away some of women's reproductive rights, and then does not mention appointments again until 2016.

whether or not their decisions will be electorally costly to the executive and legislative bodies tasked with carrying them out, because resistance to implementation (or ignoring the decisions altogether) undermines their legitimacy (Bartels and Johnson 2013; Black et al. 2016; Flemming and Wood 1997; Giles et al. 2008).[15] Thus the courts take public opinion into account indirectly when gauging the likelihood their decisions will be enforced by elected political actors.

While this scholarship considers the relationship between public opinion and the courts generally, we note these are important paths for minority influence as well. First, intense minorities seek to indirectly influence policymaking in the judiciary by selecting and supporting public officials who will make favorable judicial appointments, ideally "true believers" to the cause (Bawn et al. 2012). The *Dobbs* decision is a consequence of this indirect path to minority influence. When campaigning for office in 2016, Donald Trump made a commitment to appoint conservative judges to federal courts. He released lists of potential nominees to signal his intent to follow through, and three justices from these lists – Gorsuch, Kavanaugh, and Coney Barrett – are now seated on the Supreme Court. Beyond this, Trump appointed 226 federal judges during his presidency, amounting to about one of every four federal judges currently seated (Gramlich 2021). Second, the nature of intense minorities makes them more likely to be electorally mobilized by the Court's decisions compared to a more diffuse and inattentive majority. As a result, opinions of intense minorities likely play an outsized role in the Court's decision-making process when they are weighing the electoral costs of enforcing and implementing their decisions.

Next, we focus on the role of the federal courts, particularly the Supreme Court, in producing abortion policies and frustrated majorities. While significant policymaking efforts have occurred at the state level, the ability of states to implement these laws has depended on Supreme Court review. At the federal level, the Supreme Court has been more active in shaping abortion policies than Congress or the president. Looking at the evolution of the Supreme Court rulings on abortion and how electoral politics impacted the Court is critical to understanding how abortion policies became misaligned with public opinion prior to the *Dobbs* decision.

The *Roe v. Wade* Decision

The *Roe v. Wade* decision was preceded by two important cases involving contraception rights that laid the legal foundation for the constitutional protection of abortion rights. In *Griswold v. Connecticut* (1965), the Supreme Court

---

[15] Presidents Eisenhower and Kennedy both opted to use the power of their office to enforce Supreme Court decisions regarding school desegregation, but reportedly struggled with the decision because they knew it would hurt them electorally (Rosenberg 2008).

ruled that state restrictions on the use of birth control by married couples violated their right to privacy established in the First, Third, Fourth, and Ninth Amendments to the US Constitution. Seven years later, in *Eisenstadt v. Baird* (1972), the Supreme Court ruled that a Massachusetts state law distinguishing between married and unmarried individuals' ability to obtain contraceptives failed the rational basis test of the Fourteenth Amendment. A year later, the Court issued a decision in *Roe v. Wade* (1973), ruling that abortion is a fundamental right protected by the right to privacy rooted in the Due Process Clause of the Fourteenth Amendment.

In the *Roe* decision, the Court set up the trimester framework that shaped abortion legislation at the state and federal levels. *Roe* prohibited states from restricting abortion rights during the first trimester, leaving the decision between the patient and their doctor. The Court allowed states to regulate abortion rights in the interest of a woman's health in the second trimester and to protect the fetus in the third trimester. Because the Court ruled that abortion was a fundamental right, all restrictions on abortion were subject to strict scrutiny and must be accomplished by the least restrictive means until the third trimester. As noted prior, the decision in *Roe* closely mirrored public attitudes toward abortion, maintaining that abortion should be legal within limits structured by the circumstances and progression of a pregnancy (Rosenberg 2008).

The *Roe* decision marked the start of the modern era of abortion politics in the United States. Figure 1 depicts significant events linked to abortion politics and policy starting with the *Griswold* case and extending to *Dobbs*. This figure is far from a comprehensive list of abortion-related events from the past fifty years. We focus on select events critical to understanding changes in abortion policy between the *Roe v. Wade* and *Dobbs v. Jackson* decisions. In particular, we highlight events related to key court cases, elections, and the changing composition of the Supreme Court. In the sections that follow, we provide some context around these critical events.

The Response to *Roe*

Roe v. Wade ignited social movements in support of and opposition to abortion rights. These movements would spend the next half-century responding to each other's efforts (Banaszak and Ondercin 2016; Wilson 2013). Many of the major abortion rights organizations predated *Roe*, including Planned Parenthood (founded in1916) and the National Association for the Repeal of Abortion Laws (NARAL, founded in 1969). These groups shifted focus to fight

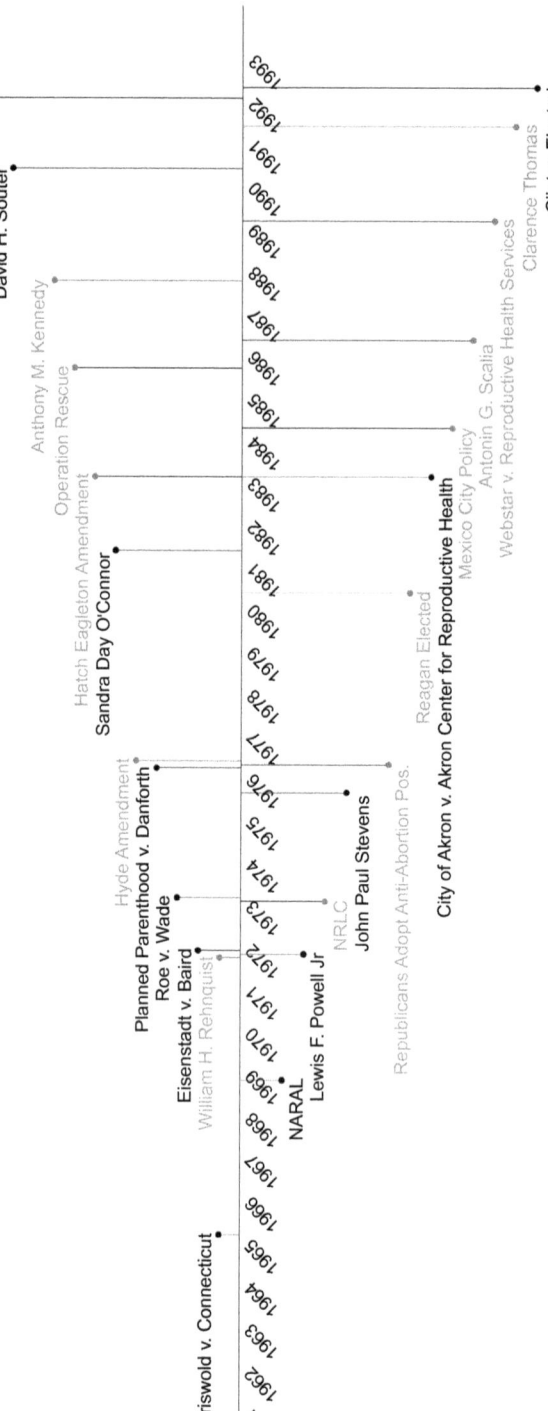

Figure 1 Timeline of abortion events, 1965–2022

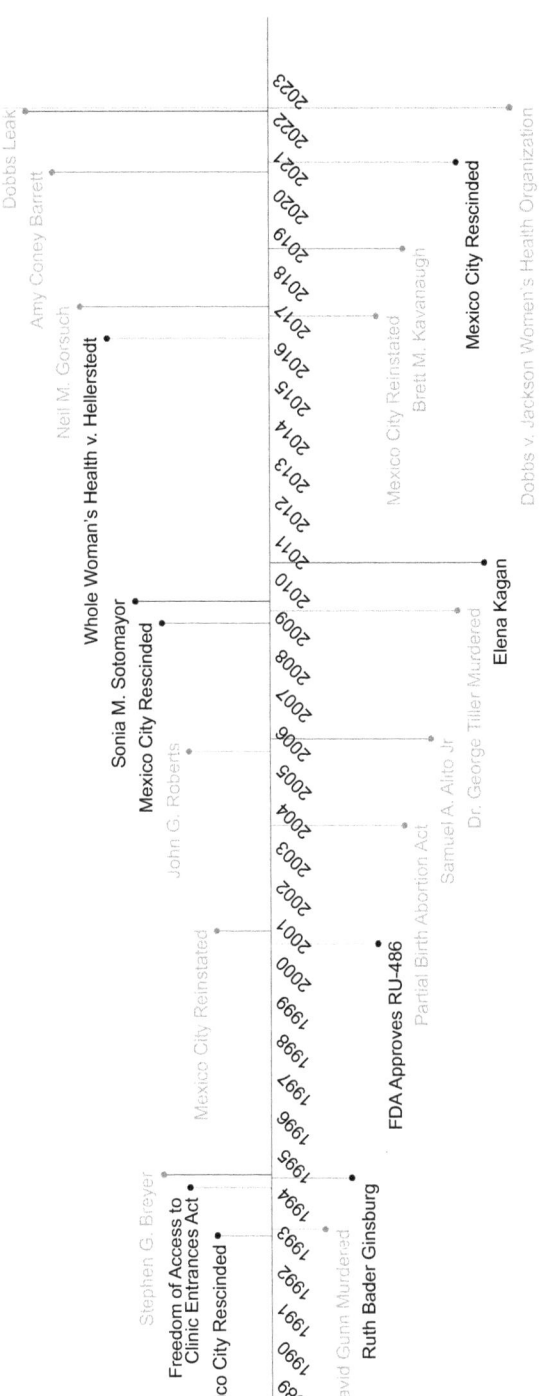

Figure 1 (cont.)

challenges to *Roe*.[16] Before *Roe*, the Catholic Church represented the most significant organization opposed to abortion rights. Afterward, a larger and more organized anti-abortion movement formed, encompassing multiple groups and interests (Haugeberg 2017).

Many activists opposed to abortion took absolutist positions, arguing that abortion was murder and should never be permitted. They advocated for a constitutional amendment establishing fetal personhood and banning abortion without exception (Ziegler 2020). Several such amendments, often called "human life amendments," have been proposed in Congress since the 1970s, and they have occasionally been advanced to the hearing stage by the Senate Judiciary Committee. In 1983, the Eagleton Hatch Amendment was the first and (to date) only human life amendment to come to a vote in the Senate. While the amendment failed 49–50, there was considerable bipartisan support for its passage, with 34 Republicans and 15 Democrats voting in favor of it (GovTrack.us 1983). Despite the lack of success, pursuit of a constitutional amendment banning abortion remains on the Republican Party platform and a focal point of the agenda for many opponents of abortion rights.

The anti-abortion movement was unsuccessful in amending the US Constitution to ban abortion, in part because a total ban was not supported by public opinion. As we will discuss in Section 4, since the passage of *Roe*, fewer than 15 percent of Americans have thought that abortion should never be permitted. As such, many members of the anti-abortion movement successfully adopted a more incremental approach, working to pass state laws regulating and limiting access to abortion (Ziegler 2020). These restrictions focused on requirements such as parental notification, waiting periods, mandated counseling, and greater regulation of doctors and facilities that conducted abortions. These incremental regulatory changes were easier for abortion rights opponents to achieve in the absence of broad public support for a total ban. They became the focus of court battles that tested just how much states could regulate abortion. And, many of these policies were essentially trial balloons for legal arguments that might ultimately overturn *Roe*.

Abortion rights advocates challenged these restrictions, claiming they were unconstitutional and countermanded the precedent set in *Roe*. In some cases, they were successful, and the Supreme Court struck down the regulations. For

---

[16] NARAL has gone through multiple name changes and rebranding. In 1973, it changed its name to the National Abortion Rights Action League. In 1993, reflecting an expansion of its mission, the organization's name changed to National Abortion and Reproductive Rights Action League. In 2003, it adopted the name NARAL Pro-Choice America. Most recently, it has changed its name to Reproductive Freedom for All (Reproductive Freedom for All 2024).

example, in 1978 Akron, Ohio passed an ordinance that sought to restrict abortion access by imposing a series of new requirements including: all abortions after the first trimester must be performed in hospitals, parental consent for minors seeking an abortion, mandatory counseling, a waiting period, and the disposal of fetal remains in a "humane and sanitary manner." Many anti-abortion groups viewed the Akron law as a potential model that could be used elsewhere to limit access to abortion more broadly (Ziegler 2020). In *Akron v. Akron Center for Reproductive Health* (1983), the Supreme Court ruled that regulations in the Akron city ordinance were not medically necessary and thus unconstitutional because they restricted the abortion procedure to the point of potentially dissuading women from seeking an abortion.[17]

The anti-abortion rights movement was also successful in pursuing federal restrictions on the use of government funds to pay for abortion procedures. In 1976, Congress passed the Hyde Amendment, which prohibited Medicaid from financing abortions, thus tying a pregnant person's ability to obtain an abortion to their socioeconomic status. The Hyde Amendment received considerable bipartisan support in the House of Representatives, with 107 Democrats and 92 Republicans voting in favor (GovTrack.us. 1976). The Supreme Court validated its constitutionality in *Harris v. McRae* (1980), arguing that the freedom to have an abortion does not give women "a constitutional entitlement to the financial resources to avail themselves of the full range of protected choices."[18] This ruling established that although the right to an abortion was constitutionally protected, if a woman could not pay for the procedure, she could not receive one. Collectively, these victories for opponents of abortion rights represented a gradual erosion of the constitutional standard established by *Roe*.

The Shifting Political Landscape

The 1980s were a critical juncture for abortion politics in the United States. In addition to battling against abortion access in the courts, the anti-abortion movement became increasingly involved in electoral politics. This approach not only helped elect candidates committed to producing and supporting legislation that restricted abortion rights, but it also bolstered a long-term strategy to overturn *Roe v. Wade* by shifting the composition of the Supreme Court (Ziegler 2020). In the 1980 presidential election, Ronald Reagan appealed directly to newly mobilized evangelical voters with promises to end abortion and to appoint judges to the Supreme Court who opposed abortion rights. Reagan's

---

[17] The Court invalidated the section of the ordinance about the disposal of fetal remains because it was too vague.

[18] The Court affirmed the constitutionality of the Hyde Amendment in other cases as well, for example *Maher v. Roe* (1977) and *Rust v. Sullivan* (1991).

stance on abortion contributed to the growing alignment of abortion rights opponents with the Republican Party and abortion rights proponents with the Democratic Party. Reagan's victory, his close ties to the Christian Right, and his success in placing conservative judges in the federal judiciary mark a significant juncture at which abortion policy drifts away from the preferences of the public.

Presidential administrations also began using their executive powers to limit access to abortion. In 1985, Reagan established the Mexico City Policy, also known as the Global Gag Rule, through executive order. The policy required foreign nongovernmental organizations to certify that they did not perform abortions or provide information about abortion services to receive aid from the United States. When Bill Clinton was elected in 1992, he rescinded the Mexico City Policy, establishing a pattern whereby all subsequent Republican presidents adopted the policy and all subsequent Democratic presidents rescinded the policy. The back-and-forth actions of presidential administrations on the Mexico City Policy reflect the changing partisan nature of abortion politics at this time. Whereas bipartisanship was evident, for example, in the successful vote on the Hyde Amendment in the late 1970s, partisan polarization significantly curtailed that possibility moving forward (more to come on this in Section 4).

The ideological makeup of the Supreme Court also changed during the 1980s. Between 1981 and 1987, Chief Justice Burger and Justices Stewart, Douglas, and Powell – all members of the *Roe* majority – retired from the Court. In their place, President Reagan appointed conservative justices, shifting the Court's ideology to the right. The newly conservative Court proved more likely to deem state-level restrictions on abortion rights to be constitutional, representing a departure from the previous Court's rulings. For example, in *Webster v. Reproductive Health Services* (1989), the Supreme Court upheld a Missouri law that imposed new restrictions on abortion procedures, such as requiring doctors to perform tests to determine the viability of a fetus if they believed the woman seeking an abortion was 20 or more weeks pregnant, prohibiting the use of public employees and facilities to perform abortions that were not necessary to save the life of the mother, and criminalizing the use of public employees, funds, and facilities to counsel a woman to get an abortion that was not necessary to save her life. The decision weakened the precedent set in *Roe* without quite overturning it, but the impact on the policy landscape was significant. *Webster* opened the floodgates for anti-abortion legislation across the states, with over 400 bills being introduced in state legislatures the following year (Kreitzer 2015).

Not all in the anti-abortion rights movement were happy with securing incremental changes in this fashion. A growing wing of the anti-abortion movement started to take direct action against abortion providers and people seeking abortions. Sidewalk protests sprang up outside of medical facilities.

Protesters attempted to block access to clinics and sought to "counsel" women seeking abortions with the hopes of changing their minds. Founded in 1989 by Randal Terry, Operation Rescue is perhaps the best-known of these direct-action organizations (Solinger 2019). Operation Rescue often occupied and obstructed access to clinics in hopes of shutting down the facility and "rescuing" fetuses. Additionally, doctors and other clinic personnel were targeted for harassment by anti-abortion activists who made personal information (e.g., home addresses) publicly available. Some anti-abortion activists even turned to violence. The National Abortion Federation reports that in the 1990s, there were eleven murders and twenty-six attempted murders of abortion providers. Hundreds of acts of arson, bombings, acid attacks, and anthrax threats against clinics and providers were also reported during this period (National Abortion Federation 2024).

These direct-action campaigns also sparked a series of legal changes related to free-speech rights and freedom from harassment in the context of abortion (Wilson 2013). Many states passed laws creating "buffer zones" that limited how close protesters could get to facilities that provided abortion services. In 1993, the US Congress passed the Freedom to Access Clinic Entrance (FACE) Act, creating federal civil and criminal penalties for using or threatening force against abortion providers and obstructing access to abortion care (S.636).[19] The FACE Act did not fully put an end to the violence, however. In 1998, Dr. Barnett Slepian was fatally shot in his home in a suburb of Buffalo, New York. A decade later, Dr. George Tiller Jr, one of the nation's few providers of late-term abortion, was killed. Tiller had been a target of violence for several decades. In 1986, the clinic he worked at in Wichita, Kansas, was firebombed, and in 1993, he was shot while in his car. Both Buffalo and Wichita had been the sites of major direct-action campaigns by Operation Rescue.

The Changing Nature of Abortion Regulations

During the 1990s and 2000s, the Supreme Court continued to affirm the constitutionality of restrictions on abortion rights and access at both the state and federal levels. Opponents of abortion rights were hopeful the Court would overturn *Roe* when deciding *Planned Parenthood of Southeastern Pennsylvania v. Casey* (1992). Instead, the Court abandoned the trimester framework and adopted an "undue burden" standard, whereby a law would be unconstitutional

---

[19] At the time of writing, there is a concerted effort among anti-abortion activists and conservative groups to overturn the FACE Act. Senator Mike Lee (R-UT) and Representative Chip Roy (R-TX-21) have proposed legislation that would overturn this law.

if it had the "purpose or effect of placing a substantial obstacle in the path of women seeking an abortion of a nonviable fetus."[20] The undue burden standard shifted the focus of the Court's reasoning to the "costs" and "benefits" associated with abortion rather than conceptualizing abortion as a constitutional right (Ziegler 2020). When adjudicating among the various restrictions included in PA's abortion law, the Court used this undue burden standard to strike down a spousal notification requirement. At the same time, the Court upheld many other requirements, including: parental notification, a waiting period, counseling, and greater regulation of doctors and facilities that conducted abortions.

In response to *Casey*, many states passed additional restrictions on abortion providers. These Targeted Regulations of Abortion Providers or TRAP laws required abortion to be performed by doctors with admitting privileges to local hospitals or in facilities that met certain surgical standards. While often cloaked in the rhetoric of women's safety, the primary purpose of these laws was to limit access to abortions by making it too burdensome for some abortion providers to continue to operate in a state. Research suggests the laws caused many clinics to close and significantly limited women's access to abortion services (Arnold 2022; Jones and Jerman 2014).

Anti-abortion efforts at the federal level during this period focused on banning certain types of abortion procedures, typically methods used only late in pregnancy and almost exclusively in situations where the fetus and/or mother faced a fatal health threat. In 1996 and 1997, Congress passed a "partial-birth" abortion ban aimed at these procedures. President Bill Clinton vetoed the ban both times, and Congress was unable to secure the votes needed to override his decision (Rose 2007). In 2003, Congress again passed a "partial-birth" abortion ban, and this time, President George W. Bush signed it into law.[21]

While the number of regulations on abortion providers and procedures increased, the nature of abortions performed in the United States has changed over the past several decades. In 2000, the Food and Drug Administration (FDA) approved mifepristone, also called RU-486, Mifeprex, or colloquially "the abortion pill." Mifepristone, when taken with a second drug, misoprostol,

---

[20] The undue burden standard in *Casey* was different from the standard first introduced by Justice Sandra Day O'Connor in her dissenting opinion in *Akron v. Akron Center for Reproductive Health* (1983); state abortion regulations are held to strict scrutiny if they place an unfair barrier in the way of a woman seeking an abortion of an unviable fetus.

[21] "Partial-birth" generally refers to abortions occurring late in pregnancy. The laws described here have sought to ban dilation and evacuation (D&E), a procedure that medical professionals deem safer than dilation and extraction (D&X). Along with the federal ban, many states have also banned D&E. Access to the D&E procedure is not only being curtailed by the law, but fewer doctors are being trained in the procedure and many medical facilities and abortions providers do not perform the procedure.

can be used to induce an abortion up to the tenth week of pregnancy. After the initial approval of the drug, the FDA expanded access by allowing it to be dispensed by pharmacies and sent via mail. Previously, a pregnant person would have to go to a doctor's office to receive the medication and receive follow-up care in person as well. Under the new FDA rules, pregnant persons could have a safe abortion in their homes (FDA Questions and Answers 2023). The use of medication abortions increased considerably during the COVID-19 pandemic. In 2023, they accounted for 65 percent of all abortions in the United States (Sanger-Katz and Miller 2024). A case concerning the continued legality of supplying abortion medication by mail is currently pending at the Supreme Court.

Changes in the Composition of the Supreme Court

Circumstances conspired to present President Donald Trump with a unique opportunity to shape the Supreme Court during his 1st administration. Presidents often have only very limited influence over the ideological composition of the Court; the small number of seats and lifetime appointments translates to limited turnover. But President Trump successfully nominated three conservative justices and paved the path to the *Dobbs* decision, which would overturn the constitutional standard established in *Roe*.

Ten months before the 2016 presidential election, conservative Supreme Court Justice Antonin Scalia passed away. President Obama announced US Court of Appeals judge Merrick Garland for the vacancy, but Senate Majority leader Mitch McConnell (R-KY) blocked Garland's appointment, leaving the seat vacant until after the election (Elving 2018). Once in office, President Trump fulfilled his campaign promise to appoint Supreme Court justices amenable to overturning *Roe*, selecting Neil Gorsuch to replace Scalia. When moderate Justice Anthony Kennedy resigned in 2018, President Trump successfully nominated conservative Brett Kavanaugh, shifting the ideological median of the Court to the right (Jessee et al. 2022). Then, in 2020, liberal Justice Ruth Bader Ginsberg passed away, and President Trump appointed Amy Coney Barrett to fill the vacancy (VanSickle-Ward et al. 2023). With Coney Barrett's appointment, the Court's ideological median shifted considerably further to the right (Jessee et al. 2022).

Less than two years later, the Court issued its decision in *Dobbs v. Jackson Women's Health Organization*, overturning *Roe v. Wade* and allowing states to set abortion policy. The case dealt with the Mississippi Gestational Act, which prohibited abortion after the fifteenth week of pregnancy. In a 6–3 decision, the Court upheld the law, overruling the precedents set in *Casey* and *Roe*. In their decision, the Court ruled that there was no constitutional right to abortion because the Constitution does not mention abortion, because abortion is not rooted deeply in the nation's history, and because it is not an essential component of "ordered liberty." The decision was hailed as a major victory for opponents of abortion, an intense minority whose long-game strategy involving the Supreme Court had finally paid off.

Yet *Dobbs* only is the first of many cases related to abortion that will appear before the Court. As noted previously, the Supreme Court will soon issue a ruling in *U.S. Food and Drug Administration v. Alliance for Hippocratic Medicine*, a case involving the legality of dispensing medication abortion through the mail. In another pending case, *Moyle v. United States*, the Court will determine whether Idaho's abortion ban violates the federal Emergency Medical Treatment and Labor Act (EMTALA). EMTALA requires that any medically unstable patient entering an emergency department be stabilized or transferred to a facility capable of stabilizing them, regardless of their ability to pay. The Court will determine whether this law applies to pregnant women who require an emergency abortion to stabilize their condition. At present, Idaho's abortion ban permits abortion when required to save the life of a pregnant woman, but not to prevent her health from deteriorating, and this is true of abortion bans in other states as well (Belluck 2024). In these and other cases, the Court will exert a significant and lasting influence on American abortion policy.

Conclusion

This brief history of abortion politics in the United States shows the influence of an intense minority on policy post-*Roe*. The creation of a constitutional basis for abortion rights sparked an active movement against abortion that worked to elect candidates and secure judicial appointments committed to reversing *Roe*. Though only a minority of Americans wanted to see abortion banned outright, this minority pursued its goals intently and was successful at securing incremental but substantial policy change over time. This outcome is consistent with intensity theory (Hill 2022), which posits that minorities can succeed in frustrating majority opinion by maximizing the electoral incentives facing political elites (in this case, elites in the Republican Party). Ultimately, abortion rights opponents succeeded in securing the Supreme Court appointments needed to overturn *Roe*, fundamentally altering abortion policy in the United States. In the next section, we turn to the impact of *Dobbs* on policy in the states and explore the concept of frustrated majorities sub-nationally.

3 State Variation in Abortion Policy Post-*Dobbs*

Kate Cox, a mother of two excited about expanding her family, was about eighteen weeks pregnant when her fetus was diagnosed with Trisomy-18. Cox's doctor explained that this condition would likely prove fatal to her fetus, but it also posed a health risk to Cox herself and endangered her future fertility.[22] After several trips to the emergency department for pregnancy-related complications, Cox, in consultation with her doctor, decided to terminate the pregnancy (Goodman 2023a). This wasn't a straightforward endeavor because Cox lived in Texas, one of the thirteen states with a trigger law that went into effect after the *Dobbs* decision. The Texas law stipulated that abortion was only legal when a pregnancy posed a serious threat to the health or life of a pregnant woman.

Cox's doctor felt that her pregnancy met these conditions but was concerned that ambiguity in the law regarding what constitutes a serious health threat would open her and any medical facility offering her privileges to professional repercussions, civil penalties, and even criminal prosecution. At the time, medical professionals convicted of violating the ban and performing an abortion illegally in the state of Texas faced a prison term of up to ninety-nine years and fines starting at $100,000 (Texas Penal Code 2023). Cox and her doctor asked a court to preauthorize the procedure to avoid these potentially severe consequences. The preauthorization was granted but faced an immediate challenge from the state's Attorney General, who threatened local hospitals with legal action and invoked the judgment of the state's Supreme Court. As she awaited the court's judgment, Cox's health continued to deteriorate, and she ultimately traveled out of state to terminate the pregnancy. When the Texas Supreme Court did eventually issue its ruling, it found that Cox's medical circumstances did not qualify her to receive an abortion under the medical exemption to the state ban.

Kate Cox's case is not unique. In a separate lawsuit, twenty-two plaintiffs, twenty of whom were denied abortion as necessary medical care, sued the state of Texas, asking the law to be clarified (Center for Reproductive Rights 2023b). These women either received abortions out of state or were forced to carry nonviable pregnancies, suffering severe medical complications and trauma as a result. The stories of these women demonstrate that even when exceptions are included in abortion law, the threat of criminal and civil penalties, ambiguity about what constitutes a "reasonable medical judgment," and the level of scrutiny such judgments tend to face create significant obstacles for women

---

[22] In the 5 percent of cases when a fetus does survive until full term, less than 10 percent survive one year due to complications of delayed organ growth and congenital heart conditions associated with Trisomy-18 (also known as Edwards syndrome).

seeking an abortion.[23] These issues are not limited to Texas; when the *Dobbs* decision returned abortion policy to the states, it created a complex and confusing policy environment for women and their doctors (Romo 2023).

In this section, we look at how *Dobbs* has reshaped the abortion policy landscape in the United States and whether these changes align with public preferences. In the case of Texas, survey data suggest that the new abortion law does not reflect the position of most Texans. Several surveys conducted after the *Dobbs* decision find that a majority of Texans support abortion in a broad set of circumstances beyond fatal health risks to a pregnant person (Brady et al. 2023; Henson and Blank 2022; PerryUndam 2022). And support is even higher for some exceptions not currently permitted by law. For instance, in a September 2021 Quinnipiac poll, nearly 80 of registered voters in Texas supported legal abortion when a pregnancy results from rape or incest, including 66 percent of registered Republicans (Quinnipiac 2021). A recent report from Public Religion Research Institute (2024) suggests that this disconnect may be commonplace, even in conservative states, and our analysis, reported next, reaches a similar conclusion. *Dobbs* has created a more complex policy environment, but not one better aligned with public opinion at the state level.

Public Opinion and Abortion Policy in the States Pre- and Post-*Dobbs*

Dobbs created a frustrated majority from a national perspective, given that a majority of Americans did not support the Supreme Court's decision to overturn *Roe*. One argument in favor of shifting policymaking responsibility to the states was the potential for improved representation at the state level. Policy congruence – the match between public opinion and policy – might be improved under a more distributed policy model. The Court anticipated increased variation in policy across the states. In the majority decision, Justice Alito wrote, "the people of the various States may evaluate those interests differently. In some States, voters may believe that the abortion right should be even more extensive than the right that *Roe* and *Casey* recognized. Voters in other States may wish to impose tight restrictions based on their belief that abortion destroys an 'unborn human being'." The Court's reasoning suggests that these policies would shift to reflect voters' preferences across states, potentially resulting in greater alignment between public opinion and policy.

---

[23] For more discussion of the implications of this case for the future of abortion rights in Texas and states with similar laws, see Goodman (2023b). In May of 2024, the Texas Supreme Court overturned the temporary injunction resulting from this lawsuit. In its ruling, the court reiterated that Texas law permits "life-saving abortions," and clarified that a person could not receive an abortion in situations where a fetus had a fatal condition unless the pregnant person's life was also at risk. Beyond this, the decision offered little clarification for women and doctors (Zernike 2024a).

Research on the alignment of public opinion with policy at the state level has yielded mixed results. Unsurprisingly, more conservative states tend to pass more conservative policies on average, whereas more liberal states tend to pass more liberal policies, suggesting policy tracks the ideological orientation of state residents (Erikson et al. 1993). However, a closer look at specific policies uncovers considerable variation in how closely various policies match the average voter's preferences (Caughey and Warshaw 2022; Lax and Phillips 2012). For instance, research on abortion policy specifically uncovered mixed evidence of policy congruence prior to *Dobbs* (Camobreco and Barnello 2008; Caughey and Warshaw 2022; Gerber 1996; Kreitzer 2015; Lax and Phillips 2012; Norrander 2001; Norrander and Wilcox 1999). But, it's important to recognize that much of this research was conducted in a constrained policy environment, meaning that states were limited in the types of policies they could implement due to the constitutional standard imposed by *Roe* (Kastellec 2018).[24] These studies of abortion policy congruence focused on policies like parental notification, public funding of abortion, waiting periods, and mandatory counseling, rather than the more extensive restrictions and bans permitted under *Dobbs*.[25]

Has *Dobbs* improved the congruence between public opinion and public policy in some states? First, it's clear that *Dobbs* changed the policy landscape significantly. Figure 2 illustrates the variation in abortion policies across states post-*Dobbs*. We use the coding scheme developed by The Center for Reproductive Rights, which classifies state laws into five categories: expanded protection, protected, not protected, hostile, and illegal. The number of states falling into each category is reported in the figure legend. As of April 2024, abortion rights were not protected in twenty-eight of fifty states. In the remaining twenty-two states, eleven offered legal protections for abortion rights, and eleven offered expanded protections.

Expanded protection states responded to *Dobbs* by enacting further protections for reproductive rights. For example, the Minnesota Supreme Court ruled that abortion was protected by the state constitution and passed statutory protections for abortion rights (Minnesota Department of Health 2023). States that are labeled as *protecting abortion* have either state laws or state constitutions that guarantee access to abortion. This category includes states like Delaware, which, in anticipation of the *Dobbs* decision, repealed its pre-*Roe* abortion ban (Center for Reproductive Rights 2024).

In the third category of states, *not protected*, abortion remains legal and accessible, but there are no state laws or constitutional protections for

---

[24] Studies of public opinion and policy congruence are shaped by the availability of public opinion data. The post-*Roe* policy environment also shaped which abortion policies were asked about and used in this analysis.
[25] The only type of abortion bans examined in these studies were "partial-birth" abortion bans.

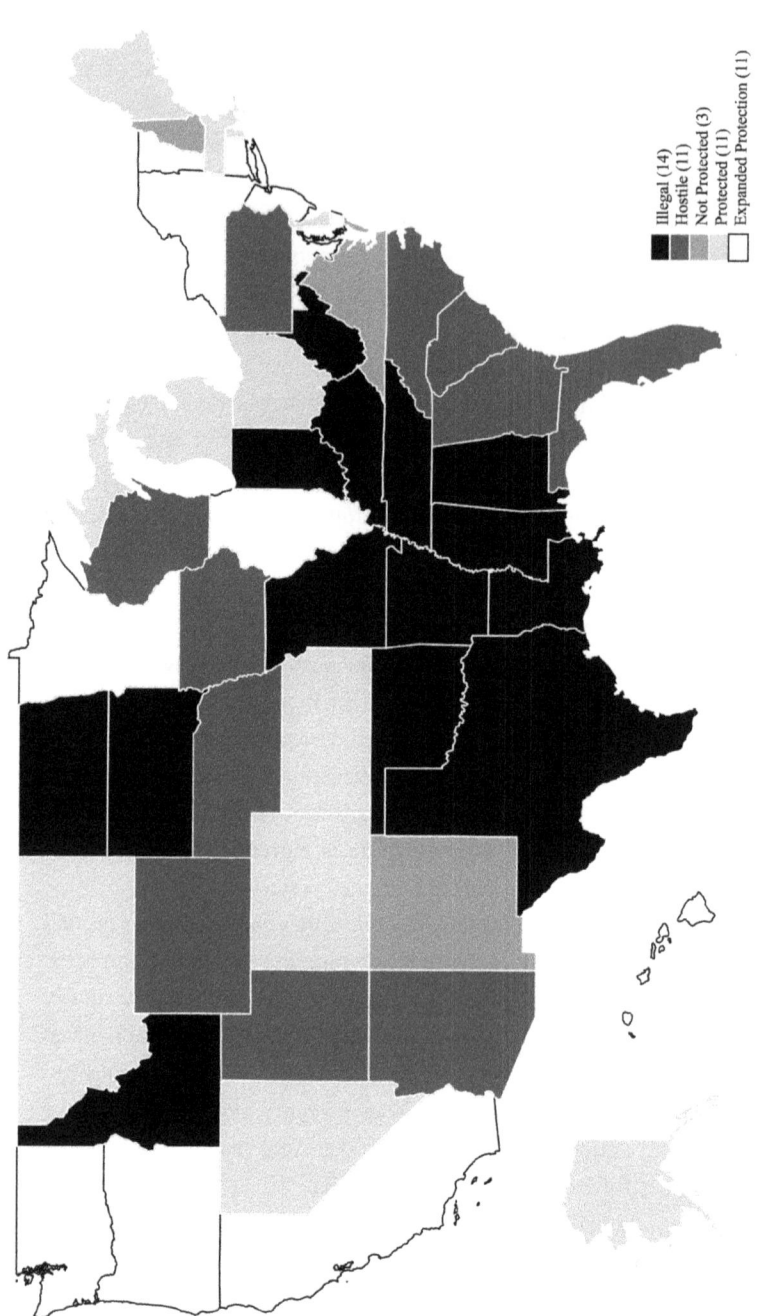

Figure 2 Abortion policies in the states, 2024

Updated 04/29/2024

reproductive rights. This category includes states like New Mexico and Virginia. The lack of protections in these states places abortion rights in a precarious position. For example, while we were working on this Element, Virginia held state legislative elections in 2023. Republicans signaled that if they were able to take control of the legislature, they would institute some form of abortion restrictions and possibly an outright ban (Romero 2023). Democrats won control of both the Virginia House and Senate, and abortion remains legal and accessible in the state for the time being (Rankin 2023).

The next two categories represent states where abortion is either highly restricted (hostile) or where abortion is banned (illegal). States classified as *hostile* to abortion rights have enacted laws that severely limit the legality of abortion or taken actions indicating severe limitations are likely to be enacted soon. And states where abortion is *illegal* have instituted complete bans or bans with very limited exceptions. Several of these states, like North Dakota and Texas, had already passed laws banning abortion before *Roe* or "trigger laws" that banned abortion immediately once *Roe* was overturned (Nash and Guarnieri 2022). In some of these states, the legality of the abortion ban is in dispute. For example, West Virginia has a pre-*Roe* ban, but there is currently an injunction against enforcement (Center for Reproductive Rights 2024).

Does abortion policy under *Dobbs* reflect greater congruence between public opinion and policy? To answer this question, we needed to identify a reliable measure of state-level opinion on abortion. Public opinion can be difficult to measure at the state level because most surveys are designed to estimate the attitudes of the US population rather than accurately represent the views of Americans living in specific states. As a result, even surveys with a large number of respondents may only interview a handful of people within many states. To address methodological challenges associated with estimating state-level opinion, Caughey and Warshaw (2022) developed a technique that leverages information across multiple surveys in a policy area. This method produces an estimate of state-level opinion and confidence intervals representing a range of uncertainty around the estimate, meaning that the true level of support for a policy in a state likely falls somewhere within that range of values. Jacob Grumbach used this technique to estimate state-level support for abortion rights in 2021, the year before the Supreme Court delivered the Dobbs decision (Grumbach 2022).[26]

---

[26] Grumbach's estimates are based on all publicly available national public opinion survey questions about abortion whose responses could be split into the categories "always legal" or support for full bans or bans with a narrow exception to preserve the life of a mother. We thank Jacob Grumbach for sharing this data with us. For more technical details on the estimation procedure used to create this measure, see Chapter 2 of Caughey and Warshaw (2022).

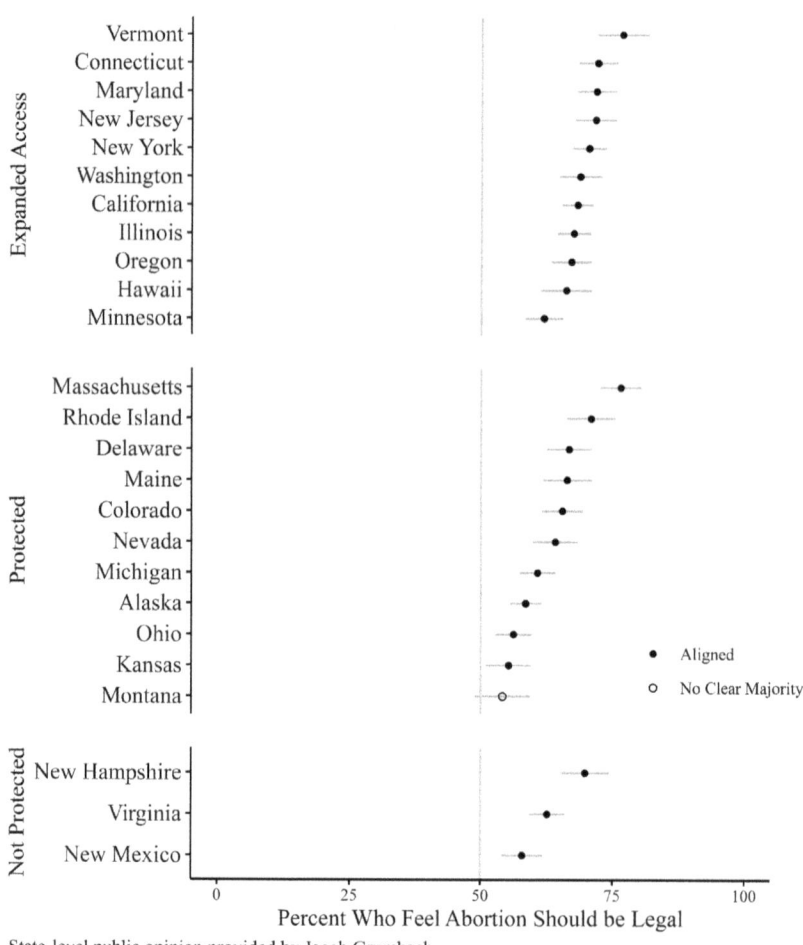

State-level public opinion provided by Jacob Grumbach

Figure 3 State-level public opinion, 2021

To assess whether policy is congruent with opinion, we plotted the percentage of each state's population who support legal abortion in Figure 3. States are clustered into categories based on the classification strategy from the Center for Reproductive Rights described above: expanded protection, protected, not protected, hostile, and illegal. Solid circles represent states where policy and opinion align. Open circles represent states where there is not a clear majority viewpoint because the confidence interval indicates the state is closely divided on the issue (approximately 50:50). Because we can't clearly identify a majority opinion, we can't assess whether opinion and policy are aligned. Asterisks represent states where public opinion and public policy are misaligned.

We find there are high levels of alignment between the public's preferences and abortion policy in states that have expanded protections, states where

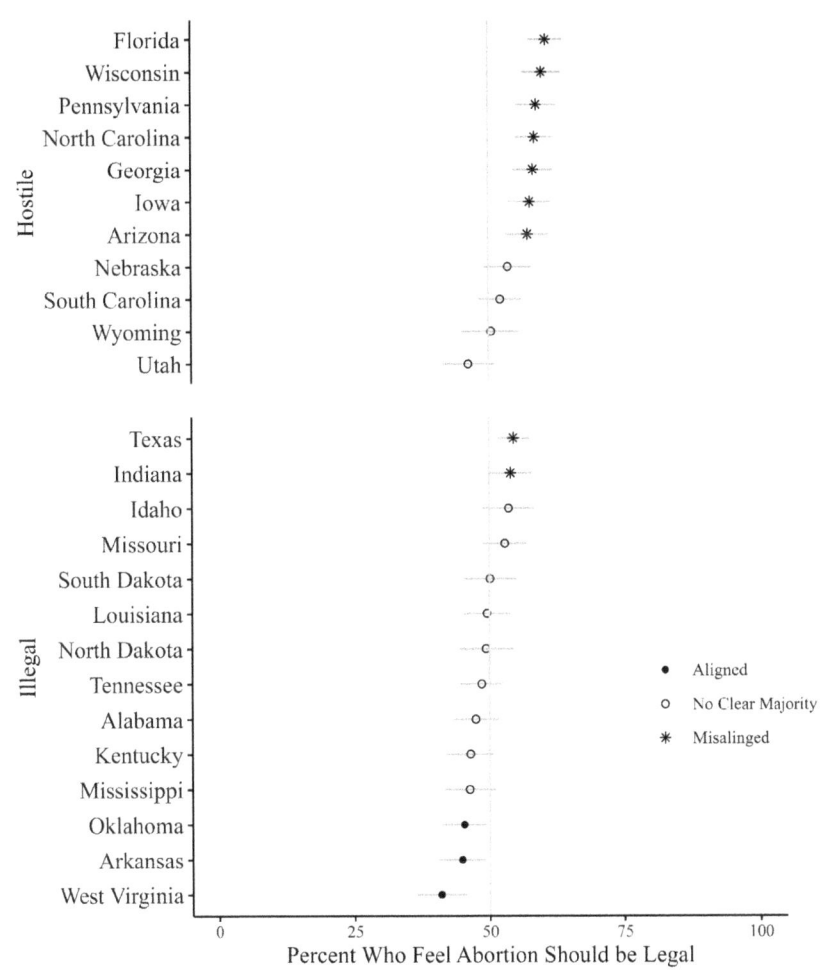

Abortion Attitudes and Polarization in the American Electorate

Hostile

State	Percent
Florida	*
Wisconsin	*
Pennsylvania	*
North Carolina	*
Georgia	*
Iowa	*
Arizona	*
Nebraska	○
South Carolina	○
Wyoming	○
Utah	○

Illegal

State	Percent
Texas	*
Indiana	*
Idaho	○
Missouri	○
South Dakota	○
Louisiana	○
North Dakota	○
Tennessee	○
Alabama	○
Kentucky	○
Mississippi	○
Oklahoma	●
Arkansas	●
West Virginia	●

Legend: ● Aligned, ○ No Clear Majority, * Misalinged

Percent Who Feel Abortion Should be Legal

State-level public opinion provided by Jacob Grumbach

Figure 3 (cont.)

abortion rights are protected, and states where abortion remains legal but is not otherwise protected. Montana is something of an outlier in that abortion is protected, but majority opinion is unclear. In this case, the Montana State Supreme Court interpreted the state constitution as protecting reproductive rights (Center for Reproductive Rights 2024). This example demonstrates that the alignment of policy and opinion is not always due to the work of legislators. In Kansas, the State Supreme Court ruled in 2019 that the state constitution protects a pregnant person's right to personal autonomy. In response to the Court's decision, the Kansas state legislature introduced a ballot measure and asked voters in the next election to clarify that the state constitution does not protect abortion rights. Voters soundly defeated this measure, with 59 percent voting no (Lysen et al. 2022). Ballot initiatives also checked a rightward shift on abortion policy from state legislatures in Nevada and Ohio.

On the other hand, there is considerable misalignment between opinion and policy among states with hostile abortion laws. Policy and opinion are misaligned in seven of these eleven states. These states reflect several examples of how policy has become increasingly misaligned by government action after the *Dobbs* decision. For example, in North Carolina, abortion was legal and available up until the twentieth week of pregnancy or later under certain circumstances. In May of 2023, state legislators passed a bill that banned abortion after the 12th week of pregnancy. Although the Democratic governor vetoed the bill, Republicans held a super-majority in the state legislature and overrode it (Harrison 2023).[27]

We cannot confidently determine the majority position in the remaining four hostile states; the point estimates in three of the four suggest that over 50 percent of the state's population supports legal abortion, which points toward misalignment, but the confidence intervals indicate these states are very closely divided on the issue. Finally, among the fourteen states where abortion is illegal, there are only three states where we can confidently say that opinion and policy are in alignment. In Oklahoma, Arkansas, and West Virginia, a clear majority of state residents oppose abortion. In two of states where abortion is illegal, Texas and Indiana, it's clear that opinion and policy are misaligned. But for the remaining nine states, the public is narrowly divided on abortion rights, and there is no clear majority.

Legislating the Timeframe around Abortion Rights

Specifying a timeframe around abortion rights has been an ongoing dimension of policymaking since the early 1990s, with states testing how far they can restrict abortion after the Casey decision removed the trimester framework laid out in *Roe*. Now that *Roe* has been overturned, the focus on timing has sharpened. For instance, "fetal heartbeat bills" banning abortion at six weeks (two weeks after a woman's missed period) have been introduced and passed in several states, though some of these laws face ongoing court injunctions keeping them from taking effect (Smyth 2022). Timing is also a feature of policymaking efforts at the federal level. As we noted in the introduction to this Element, Senator Lindsey Graham (R-SC) introduced a fifteen-week federal abortion ban just prior to the 2022 midterm elections. The ban was intended to further mobilize Republican voters around the issue of abortion in order to counteract Democratic mobilization around the *Dobbs* decision, though it was not especially well received (Allen et al. 2022).

---

[27] In April of 2023, Tricia Cotham switched party affiliation from Democrat to Republican, providing the Republican Party with the veto-proof supermajority in the state legislature.

Recently collected survey data further highlight the disconnect between public opinion and state policy imposing a narrow timeframe, as well as the unpopularity of proposals like the fifteen-week federal ban. The 2022 American National Election Pilot Study, administered after the *Dobbs* decision, asked questions about whether Americans supported abortion in various circumstances (any reason, serious birth defect, rape or incest, and fatal health risk to the mother) and under various timeframes (never, first trimester only, first and second trimesters only, and in all three trimesters). For context, most abortions occur early in pregnancy, largely due to the increased accessibility of medication abortion. In the United States, about nine in ten abortions take place within the first twelve weeks of pregnancy – the first trimester (Popinchalk and Sedgh 2019).

The figures in Table 1 highlight that both timing and circumstance intersect to shape public opinion about abortion rights. Among Democrats, support for abortion is fairly high, often throughout pregnancy for circumstances generally

Table 1 Support for abortion in various circumstances by trimester, 2022

	Democrats	Independents	Republicans
Fatal Risk to the Mother			
Never	3.36	15.52	15.87
1st trimester	16.46	17.88	33.89
1st–2nd trimesters	12.99	15.56	14.50
1st–3rd trimesters	67.19	51.04	35.74
Serious Birth Defect			
Never	6.35	20.76	34.44
1st trimester	17.51	23.71	34.45
1st–2nd trimesters	21.19	17.34	13.74
1st–3rd trimesters	54.95	38.2	17.37
Rape or Incest			
Never	3.97	16.06	20.83
1st trimester	20.48	29.34	47.57
1st–2nd trimesters	22.6	14.34	15.08
1st–3rd trimesters	52.95	40.26	16.52
Any Reason			
Never	14.65	31.12	61.22
1st trimester	27.01	32.32	29.22
1st–2nd trimesters	30.48	14.77	5.60
1st–3rd trimesters	27.85	21.79	3.97

Note: Data are from the 2022 ANES Pilot Study. Entries are percentages and survey weights are applied.

thought to be beyond women's control – sexual violence, fatal risk to the mother, and fetal defects. Support is more variable when Democrats are asked about the legality of abortion for "any reason," though a majority support abortion for "any reason" in both the first and second trimesters. Among Republicans, the picture is a bit more complex. A majority of Republicans, 61 percent, think abortion "for any reason" should never be legal. However, clear majorities of Republicans support legal abortion in the three circumstances beyond women's control – at least early on in pregnancy – with nontrivial portions of the party allowing for abortion past the first trimester as well. When pregnant women face a fatal health risk, only about 16 percent of Republicans think abortion should never be permitted at any stage of the pregnancy.

The opening anecdote of this section illustrates how difficult it can be for women to obtain an abortion even when their circumstances ostensibly exempt them from restrictive policies. Kate Cox discovered that the fetus she carried had a serious birth defect in her second trimester. The condition posed a serious and potentially fatal health threat to her as well – a situation where, according to this data, about 50 percent of Republicans and about 80 percent of Democrats would support Cox's right to an abortion. Yet, medical professionals disagreed about the extent of the threat she faced, and the state's Attorney General and court system leveraged this disagreement to deny her legal right to the procedure. Cox's story highlights not only a situation where policy does not align with public opinion, but also the way public support for abortion in some circumstances can be further undercut by exemptions that are inaccessible in practice. As states move toward increasingly restrictive policies with more narrowly defined restrictions in terms of timeframe and circumstances, this issue takes on increased significance.

Conclusion

Our analysis makes clear that in the wake of *Dobbs* states have adopted a wider range of abortion policies. Yet in many states, these policies do not align with public opinion. Misalignment is more common in states with restrictive policies, and in many of these states opinion is very closely divided, with no clear majority. But in nine states where the law is hostile to abortion rights or abortion is altogether illegal, state residents represent a frustrated majority. This amounts to about 109 million Americans or 33 percent of the US population. Another 46 million Americans live in states with no clear majority.

Lax and Phillips (2012) have found that statehouse policy is often more polarized than the electorate, and we uncover some evidence of that here as well. Without the constraint imposed by *Roe*, intense minorities, especially in Republican-controlled states, have managed to push policy to the right of the median voter. However, not much time has passed since the *Dobbs* decision, and it is possible that greater alignment will come with time, particularly if frustrated majorities become more activated or if there is an expansion in the size and effort of an intense majority in support of abortion rights. We have seen some evidence of mobilization around ballot initiatives related to abortion rights in states like Ohio and Kansas where the outcomes have served as a corrective on efforts of state legislatures to push policy further to the right of public opinion. On the other hand, twenty-four states do not have a citizen-initiated process for direct ballot measures or referenda, which limits the utility of this strategy (Ballotpedia 2024a). Further, Caughey and Warshaw (2022) have found that historically ballot initiatives have actually led to greater incongruence, usually the conservative direction. Lastly, the Supreme Court will continue to adjudicate challenges to state law, which may reinforce some efforts to restrict abortion rights beyond the preferences of state residents.

In the next section, we shift focus a bit and look more closely at public opinion toward abortion and its changing relationship to partisanship over time. We consider how abortion became a partisan issue in the decades following the *Roe* decision as a backdrop for understanding how abortion has shaped, and will continue to shape, electoral politics in times of heightened polarization. In subsequent sections, we build on these insights to identify the subset of Americans with intense preferences about abortion and outline their unique electoral behavior and the consequences for policy influence.

4 Abortion Attitudes and Partisanship in the American Electorate

The Supreme Court's decision in *Roe v. Wade* and the elite response that followed sparked changes in how Americans connected their beliefs about abortion rights to their partisan identities. Though public opinion about abortion appears relatively static in the decades that followed, significant changes were underway that led people to shift their partisan loyalties, resulting in a Democratic Party that increasingly supported abortion rights and a Republican Party that increasingly opposed them. In this section, we analyze trends in public attitudes toward abortion over time and provide evidence of growing partisan polarization. We connect these trends to the parties' efforts to appeal to voters on the basis of their abortion preferences, focusing on messaging in the party platforms to show how these appeals developed.

The process by which Americans sorted themselves into distinctive partisan camps was part of a broader process linked to ideological polarization (Hout et al., 2022; Levendusky 2009; Theriault 2008) and social group attachments (Mason 2018). Sorting produced more distinctive and homogeneous parties, and, as a consequence, it has also escalated partisan conflict (Iyengar and Westwood 2015).

Because the *Dobbs* decision represents a major policy victory for the Republican Party and a major loss for the Democratic Party, abortion has re-emerged as a focal point of partisan conflict. As a result, public opinion toward abortion is critically important for understanding contemporary partisan polarization and its impact on American elections. It is also useful for understanding minority influence on abortion policy, as an intense minority of abortion opponents came to exert a powerful influence on the Republican Party after *Roe*.

Public Support for Abortion Rights

Before the landmark *Roe v. Wade* decision, few national surveys asked about people's attitudes toward abortion, though the data that do exist point toward growing public acceptance of abortion leading up to *Roe* (Rosenberg 2008).[28] Two generalizations can be made about abortion attitudes in *Roe*'s wake. First, public opinion has remained relatively stable in the decades following *Roe*. To illustrate this point, we plotted answers to a survey question that was asked consistently on the American National Election Study (ANES) surveys between 1980 and 2022 in Figure 4. The question asked whether abortion should never be permitted, whether it should be permitted in a narrow set of cases, a broader set of cases, or always be permitted.[29]

While there is some change from survey to survey, abortion attitudes have not fluctuated dramatically over time. Melissa Deckman and her colleagues (2024) argue that offsetting demographic shifts are operating here under the surface, but the overall picture is one of stability. This is particularly true in terms of opposition to abortion rights. On average, across this period, only 12.5 percent of respondents agreed with the position that abortion should never be legally permitted, and there is very little variation from year to year. By contrast, there is somewhat more movement in the proportion of Americans who feel that abortion should always be permitted. In the 1980s, around 36 percent supported unrestricted abortion rights. By 1992, the proportion supporting unrestricted

---

[28] The General Social Survey (GSS), which asked about abortion attitudes before *Roe* in 1972 and then after the decision in 1973, recorded increased support for legalized abortion between these two time points (Smith and Son 2013). However, the American National Election Studies do not record similar movements between 1972 and 1976, the first two presidential election years in which the question is asked.

[29] The specific question wording is: "There has been some discussion about abortion during recent years. Which of the following opinions on this page best agrees with your view?" Respondents were supplied with the following choices: (1) By law, abortion should never be permitted (never permitted), (2) The law should permit abortions only in the case of rape, incest, or when the woman's life is in danger (a narrow set of cases), (3) The law should permit abortion for reasons other than rape, incest, or danger to the woman's life, but only after the need for the abortion has been clearly established (a broader set of cases), and (4) By law, a woman should always be able to obtain an abortion as a matter of personal choice. The ANES asked about abortion prior to 1980 but used a different question.

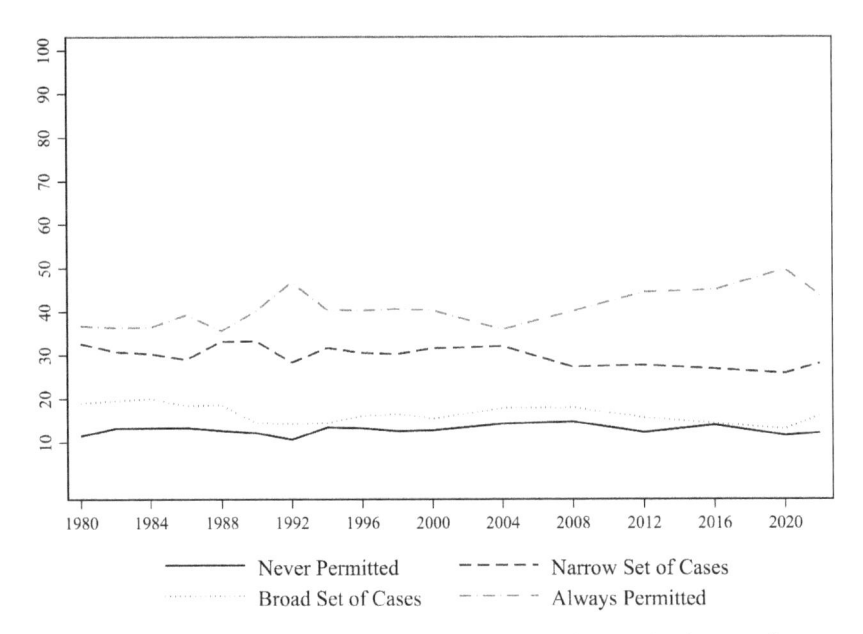

Figure 4 Abortion attitudes in the American National Election Studies, 1980–2022

access to abortion increased to about 48 percent. Support then fluctuated for a time, reaching a record high of 50 percent in 2020. These trends illustrate that the *Dobbs* decision and the changes to state laws it triggered do not reflect the preferences of a majority of Americans but rather a small and vocal minority.

A second generalization about public support for abortion rights is that efforts to measure public opinion in this area are highly dependent on the way survey researchers formulate their questions. In a comprehensive analysis of existing public opinion polling on abortion, Norrander and Wilcox (2023) find that public support for abortion rights is higher when a survey question frames abortion as a decision between a woman and her doctor compared to questions that do not explicitly mention a role for doctors. Similarly, survey questions that specify a time frame – usually a trimester or a specific number of weeks into a pregnancy – yield different results than those leaving a timeframe open-ended.

Survey questions that ask about the circumstances surrounding an abortion also reveal how dependent opinion is on question wording. For instance, questions linked to specific "traumatic" circumstances (defined in this study as a fatal health risk for the mother or fetus, rape, or incest) tend to elicit higher levels of public support compared to "social" circumstances (defined as a personal preference to not have more children, financial reasons, or being unmarried and not wishing to marry the father). These examples highlight that public opinion on abortion is nuanced, and Americans' judgments on the legality of abortion rights are highly contextual. For this reason, Norrander and Wilcox (2023) argue that the American public can best be described as "situationists," preferring abortion be legal in some situations but not others, rather than "absolutists," who prefer abortion be either outlawed or always permitted. Added to this complexity are factors like variation in preference intensity (Hill 2022) and the connections between abortion attitudes and other social and political identities, such as religious affiliation and especially partisanship (Deckman et al. 2024), which we turn to next.

The Alignment of Abortion Attitudes with Partisan Identities

In contemporary politics, one of the most influential predictors of abortion attitudes is a person's partisan identity (VanSickle-Ward and Wallsten 2019). Historically, this was not always the case. When *Roe v. Wade* was decided in 1972, attitudes about abortion did not correlate very strongly with partisan attachments, and the parties themselves did not hold very distinct positions on abortion rights (Rose 2007). The Republican Party had a moderate faction which consisted of many professional, college-educated women with feminist views who were supportive of reproductive rights. In the Democratic Party, more conservative, religious Catholics opposed abortion rights. In the years that followed *Roe*, changes within the parties led to a growing alignment of partisan identities and abortion attitudes, resulting in the distinct positions we observe today.

The growing correspondence between partisanship and abortion attitudes represents what political scientists refer to as a partisan realignment. Realignment occurs when a highly salient issue emerges that cross-pressures partisanship, such that there is disagreement among party members about which position the party should take. Elites coordinate to reach a consensus position, creating polarization and driving the parties further apart on the issue. The public responds to elite position-taking by reorganizing or sorting themselves into the party that better matches their views on the issue (Carmines and Stimson 1989; Zaller 1992). The shift in abortion positions among the political parties did not happen in a single, critical election; instead, it developed over many years, representing an "issue evolution" (Adams 1997; Wolbrecht 2000). Partisanship is generally a stable identity throughout a person's lifetime, and large-scale changes like this are relatively rare. It was not until political elites within each party united on abortion after the 1980 election that the American public began to view this issue in partisan terms (Luker 1984; Spruill 2017).

Abortion Attitudes and Polarization in the American Electorate

The evolving connection between partisanship and abortion attitudes is reflected in the party platforms.[30] In 1972, the Democratic and Republican parties wrote their platforms only a few months before the Supreme Court would hear arguments in *Roe v. Wade*, and neither party felt the issue warranted mention. The 1976 platforms tell a different story and reveal the tension the issue sparked within each party. Consider the Republican Party platform first:

> The question of **abortion** is one of the most difficult and controversial of our time. It is undoubtedly a moral and personal issue, but it also involves complex questions relating to medical science and criminal justice. There are those in our Party who favor complete support for the Supreme Court decision which permits **abortion** on demand. There are others who share sincere convictions that the Supreme Court's decision must be changed by a constitutional amendment prohibiting all **abortions.** Others have yet to take a position, or they have assumed a stance somewhere in between polar positions. We protest the Supreme Court's intrusion into the family structure through its denial of the parents' obligation and right to guide their minor children. The Republican Party favors a continuance of the public dialogue on **abortion** and supports the efforts of those who seek enactment of a constitutional amendment to restore protection of the right to life for unborn children. (Republican Party Platform 1976) (emphasis added)

Social conservatives within the Republican Party influenced two key battles over women's rights related to the 1976 platform. At the 1976 convention, a platform subcommittee voted down planks supporting the Equal Rights Amendment (ERA) and abortion. While feminists in the Republican Party were successful at reversing the subcommittee's decision on the ERA, they were less successful on abortion. In an attempt to subvert a plank supporting a constitutional amendment banning abortion, feminists at the Republican Convention gathered enough signatures to have the floor consider a proposal to strike any mention of abortion on the platform. A voice vote on this proposal failed, and the anti-abortion language remained (Freeman 1987; Wolbrecht 2000).

While considerably shorter, the 1976 Democratic Party's position on abortion similarly acknowledges competing attitudes. It takes a distinctive stance relative to the Republican Party by formalizing opposition to a constitutional amendment banning abortion:

> We fully recognize the religious and ethical nature of the concerns which many Americans have on the subject of **abortion**. We feel, however, that it is undesirable to attempt to amend the U.S. Constitution to overturn the Supreme Court decision in this area. (Democratic Party Platform 1976)

---

[30] For more detailed analysis of the evolution of the parties on women's issues, including abortion, see Wolbrecht (2000).

Both parties refined their positions between 1976 and 1980. Republican elites defeated the moderate feminist wing of the party, coalescing behind explicit opposition to abortion rights (Spruill 2017). The relevant portion of the Republican Party's platform still (briefly) acknowledges debate within the party over the issue but more strongly endorses a constitutional abortion ban.

> There can be no doubt that the question of **abortion**, despite the complex nature of its various issues, is ultimately concerned with equality of rights under the law. While we recognize differing views on this question among Americans in general – and in our own Party – we affirm our support of a constitutional amendment to restore protection of the right to life for unborn children. We also support the Congressional efforts to restrict the use of taxpayers' dollars for **abortion**. We protest the Supreme Court's intrusion into the family structure through its denial of the parent's obligation and right to guide their minor children. (Republican Party Platform 1980)

The wording also changed in the Democratic Party's platform in 1980. While retaining mention of religious and ethical concerns, the Democratic Party more clearly supported the *Roe* decision and reiterated opposition to a constitutional amendment that would overturn the Court's ruling.

> We fully recognize the religious and ethical concerns which many Americans have about **abortion**. We also recognize the belief of many Americans that a woman has a right to choose whether and when to have a child. The Democratic Party supports the 1973 Supreme Court decision on **abortion** rights as the law of the land and opposes any constitutional amendment to restrict or overturn that decision. (Democratic Party Platform 1980)

Since 1980, the Republican Party has continued to express opposition to abortion rights in their platforms, including calls for a constitutional amendment to ban abortion. Abortion has also become entwined with other issues central to the party, including foreign policy, family values, and education. Support for abortion rights has continued to be present in the Democratic Party platform as well. For the Democrats, this issue has expanded to include reproductive rights more generally and health care. A candidate's stance on abortion has become a central qualifying issue for presidential candidates from both parties (Cohen et al. 2009). The Republican Party has consistently fielded presidential candidates who take positions against abortion, and the Democratic Party has consistently fielded presidential candidates who take positions in favor of abortion rights. Elected officials and party activists have followed suit, and consensus among party elites has sent a clear signal to the public, particularly those paying attention to politics, about distinctions between the parties on abortion rights.

Abortion Attitudes and Polarization in the American Electorate 41

Elite polarization caused some members of the public to realize their abortion attitudes no longer matched the position taken by their party (Carmines and Woods 2002; Layman and Carsey 1998). People who faced this conflict tended to change their partisan affiliation to match their existing abortion attitudes instead of adjusting their abortion attitudes to match their existing party identification (Adams 1997; Killian and Wilcox 2008). For instance, in the ANES panels conducted between 1982 and 1997, pro-life Democrats were more likely than other Democrats to switch their party identification to Republican, and the same was true of pro-choice Republicans switching to the Democratic Party (Killian and Wilcox 2008). This was also evident in terms of vote choice. In the 1992 presidential election, many pro-choice Republicans defected and voted for Perot rather than the Bush–Quayle ticket. The Clinton–Gore ticket also suffered defections by pro-life Democrats, though this was less common (Abramowitz 1995).

To illustrate the changing nature of the public's abortion attitudes based on party identification, we present data from the ANES survey from 1980 to 2022 in Figure 5.[31] This figure draws on the same survey question used previously, which asked about the circumstances under which a person thinks abortion should be legal. Despite stability in aggregate opinion, there have been partisan shifts over time. The shift toward greater support for abortion rights is clear among Democrats (Panel A). In 1980, 37 percent of Democratic identifiers felt abortion should always be legal. By 2020, the proportion had nearly doubled, with 72 percent of Democrats sharing this view. Republicans (Panel C) adopted a more restrictive position during this period. In 1980, only 9 percent of Republicans felt that abortion should never be allowed. By 2022, that number has nearly doubled, with 17 percent of Republicans sharing this view. Additionally, there was a 14-point increase since 1980 in support for the position that abortions should be limited to only a narrow set of cases – that is, rape, incest, or when a pregnant woman faced a fatal health risk. The trends for independent identifiers' abortion attitudes reported in Panel B are less clear. Support for the position that abortion should be legal in all circumstances and a broad set of cases increased slightly after 2010 for this group (though the argument about elite cues and party sorting does not apply to this group, which is not as influenced by party elites).

The extent of polarization is perhaps even clearer in Figure 6, which depicts answers to the same question as in Figure 5 but plots the average response by

---

[31] Independents who "lean" toward one of the two parties are included with that partisan category in all subsequent analyses (Klar and Krupnikov 2016).

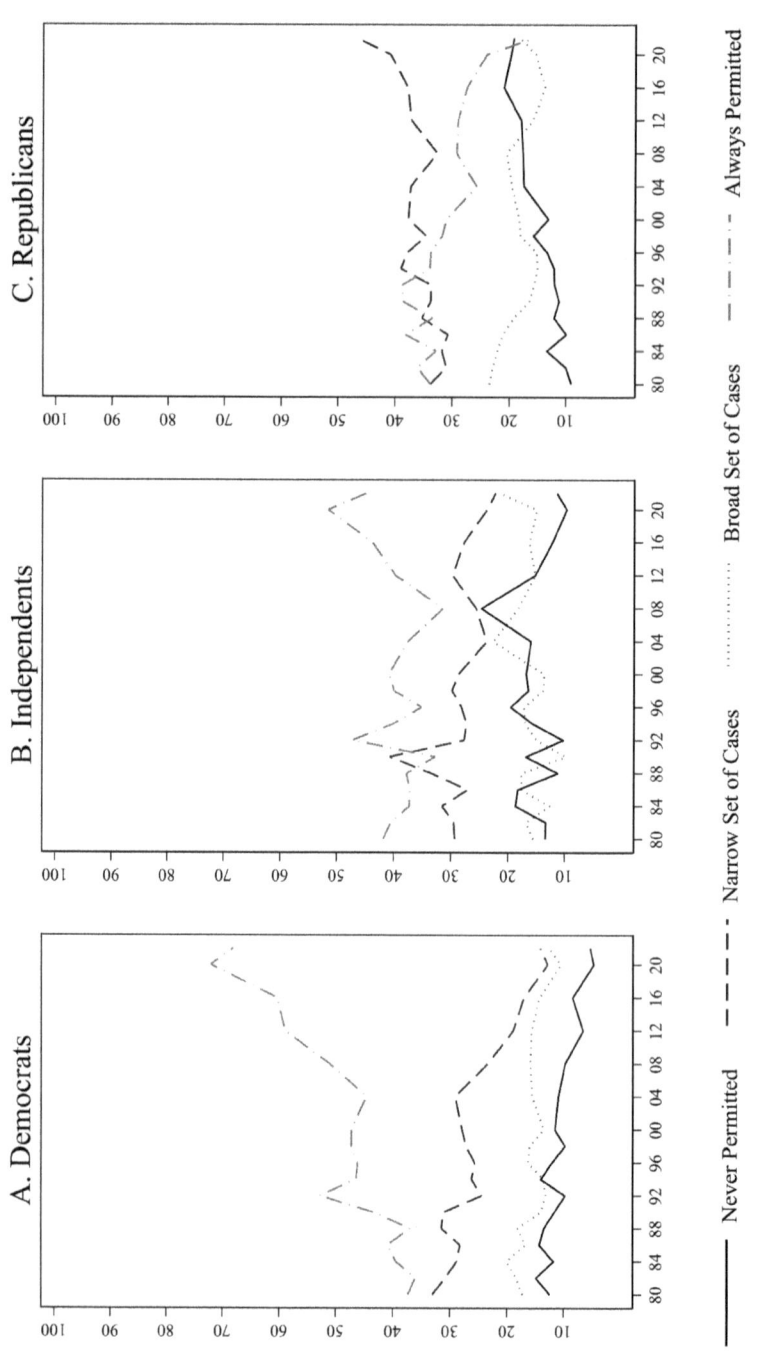

Figure 5 Abortion attitudes by political party, 1980–2022

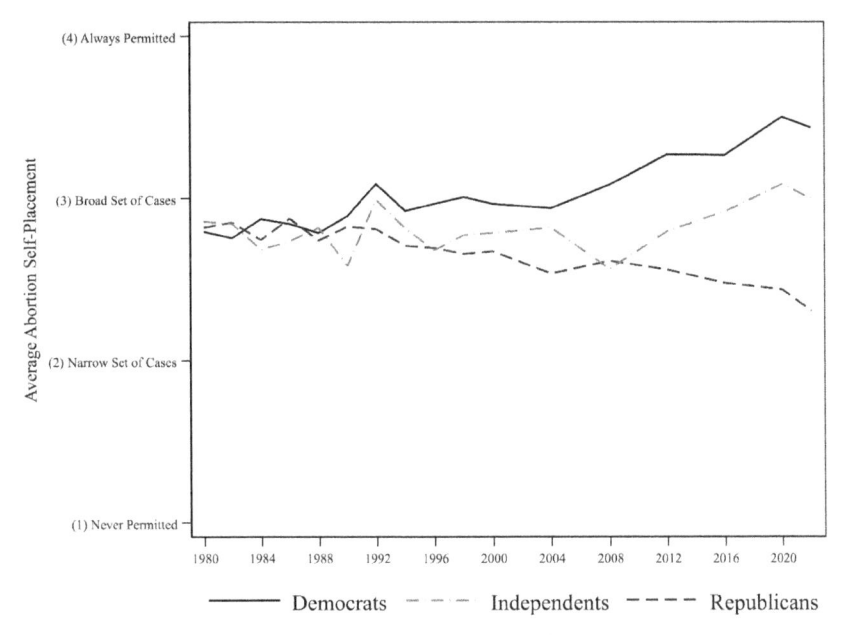

Figure 6 Average abortion attitudes by political party, 1980–2022

party over time. In 1980, there was virtually no difference between average levels of abortion support among Democrats (2.8), independents (2.9), and Republicans (2.8). Democratic and Republican attitudes on abortion began to polarize in the 1990s and have continued to grow further apart over time. In 2022, the average position on abortion for Democrats was 3.5, somewhere between abortion being legal in a broad range of circumstances and always legal. The average position for Republicans in 2022 was 2.3, indicating that the average Republican in the electorate believes that abortion should be legal in at least cases of rape, incest, and if the mother's life is in danger. Independents' attitudes about abortion fluctuate a bit more but are on a trajectory toward greater acceptance of abortion rights over time. By 2022, independents' average position on abortion was closer to Democratic identifiers than Republican identifiers.

Conclusion

Our analysis in this section shows that only a small minority of the public – about 12 percent – feels that abortion should be illegal in all circumstances. The majority of the public, by contrast, either takes a "situationist" perspective (supporting abortion in certain situations) or prefers abortion always be legal. As abortion became an increasingly partisan issue and opponents of abortion coalesced in the Republican Party after the *Roe* decision, this small, but intense, minority was able to exert disproportionate influence over abortion policy. Intensity theory (Hill 2022) suggests a mechanism for this mismatch between size and influence tied to preference intensity and political engagement. In the next section, we develop a method for capturing preference intensity and evaluate the characteristics of Americans with intense preferences – a group we call abortion-focused Americans – along with the attitudinal and behavioral correlates of preference intensity in order to better understand the impact of this group on elections and abortion policy.

5 Preference Intensity and Abortion-Focused Americans

The American National Election Studies (ANES) regularly asks people to describe things they like and dislike about the two major political parties. To get a sense of how people answer, consider two people who participated in the 2008 survey: Robert and Carol.[32] Robert is a 46-year-old white man living in the state of California. He frequently attends a mainline Protestant church and did not earn a college degree. When asked what he liked about the Democratic Party, Robert responded, "They are pro-abortion." Carol is a white woman living in North Dakota. Like Robert, she regularly attends church, though she identifies as an evangelical rather than a mainline Protestant. Carol also never went to college. When asked in 2008 what she likes about the Republican Party, Carol responded, "Most of them are pro-life, I am a one-issue voter, and I'm pro-life."

Though these survey questions do not prompt any specific criteria for evaluating the parties, both Robert and Carol spontaneously mentioned abortion. This suggests that abortion is central to their conceptualization of party politics and that both likely have intense preferences about abortion rights. The broader context of the 2008 election is also instructive. The country was experiencing one of the worst economic crises since the Great Depression, making the economy one of the most salient issues of the election. Racial progress was at the forefront of people's minds because the Democratic ticket included the party's first Black presidential nominee. For most voters, abortion was not a pressing issue (Saad 2008). But, even with everything else going on, abortion was so important to Robert and Carol that it was the first thing that came to mind when asked what they liked or disliked about the political parties.

Although Robert and Carol share a common focus on abortion, they do not share a position on abortion policy. When asked the standard question about policy positions, Robert selected: "by law, a woman should always be able to obtain an abortion as a matter of personal choice." Carol, by contrast, said the

---

[32] Robert and Carol are pseudonyms given to two respondents from the 2008 ANES.

statement "by law, abortion should never be legal" best reflected her views. Being classified as an "abortion-focused American" indicates that abortion is an important issue for these voters and that their preference intensity is high, but not that they hold any particular position on abortion.

It turns out that Americans often mention specific issues like abortion when asked to evaluate the parties, and this pattern of issue mentions tells us something meaningful about their policy priorities and preference intensity. We use this approach – identifying abortion mentions in party evaluation questions – to take a closer look at people with intense preferences on abortion, a group we refer to as "abortion-focused Americans." To better conceptualize the kinds of Americans who make this issue a priority, we identify the demographic characteristics associated with abortion focus. We also evaluate the relationship between abortion focus and partisanship, uncovering significant differences in the prevalence of abortion focus and as well as the kinds of themes people use to discuss the issue across party lines. Our ability to identify abortion-focused Americans using this approach situates us to take a closer and more careful look in the coming sections at how intensity shapes electoral behavior and whether the relationship between the two conforms to our expectations about intense and influential minorities.

Identifying Abortion-Focused Americans

Thus far, we have focused on survey questions that reveal the positions Americans take on abortion rights. However, asking questions to gauge the intensity of a person's preferences is less common and somewhat more challenging from a survey design standpoint. Some researchers have relied on questions asking about "issue importance" as an indicator of preference intensity, working from the assumption that people hold more intense preferences on issues that matter most to them. However, even when survey respondents are asked about importance directly, it can be hard to gauge relative issue priorities. For example, Ryan and Ehlinger (2023) analyzed a battery of fifteen issue importance measures from the 2008–2009 ANES panel and found that importance ratings were prone to false positives, meaning ratings tended to be uniformly quite high across issues and did not differentiate well among various issue priorities. They argued certain cognitive biases that plague survey research (e.g., acquiescence bias and social desirability bias) account for these high importance ratings. Beyond this, citizens have an incentive to exaggerate the personal importance of issues when they hold even only weak preferences in order to secure representation. As a result, simply asking people about the relative importance of various issues does not allow us to readily discern where abortion stands among people's issue priorities.

Beyond this, the ANES rarely asks respondents about the importance of abortion. In the time frame for our analysis – presidential elections from 2008 to 2020 – it is asked only once, in 2020. Absent a direct question posed consistently across election years, we faced a challenge when it comes to identifying preference intensity, evaluating its relationship to electoral behavior, and connecting our analysis with common conceptualizations of intense minority influence. To overcome this obstacle, we took advantage of abortion mentions in the open-ended party evaluation questions asked in the ANES. These issue mentions are spontaneous, and because the party evaluation questions do not mention abortion (or any other issue) explicitly, we can be confident that we obtain a relatively "clean" assessment of abortion focus that is not meaningfully influenced by question wording.[33] Essentially, this approach offers an unobtrusive and nonreactive way of assessing the weight Americans place on abortion when evaluating the parties.

In the introduction to this section, we heard from two participants in the 2008 ANES survey: Robert and Carol. Both offered relatively straightforward positions on abortion in their evaluations of the parties. But, there is considerable variation in how Americans invoke abortion. Table 2 offers a few more examples of people's answers to the open-ended party evaluation questions from the 2020 ANES. This set of responses is not intended to be representative of the full dataset, but the examples we chose highlight the kinds of abortion-related content provided spontaneously by survey respondents when asked to evaluate the parties. Some responses are focused entirely on reproductive rights, whereas others include a range of issue positions. Some include exposition on reproductive rights, whereas others merely use the pro-choice or pro-life label. The more elaborated responses reference related concepts that can be used to glean further insights into public opinion, including religion, morality, related social programs to support women and families, access to contraception, Supreme Court decisions, and time frames surrounding access to abortion services.

In a later section, we dig deeper into that content. For our present purposes, we focus simply on whether a person mentioned abortion in any of their answers to these party evaluation questions.[34] Those who did, including the survey

---

[33] For more information about the use of open-ended survey questions to gauge issue importance, see Ryan and Ehlinger's (2023) work on issue publics. See also Abramowitz (1995) for use of the ANES open-ended questions to evaluate abortion salience.

[34] Compared to the party evaluations, there were considerably fewer mentions of abortion in the candidate evaluations. On average across the four elections, only 4 percent of respondents mentioned abortion when evaluating the Democratic candidate. There is greater variation in the Republican mentions of abortion, with around 8 percent of respondents mentioning the issue when evaluating Romney in 2012 and less than 2 percent mentioning abortion when evaluating Trump in 2016. Because the issue of abortion appears to be more strongly grounded in people's perceptions of the political parties than the candidates, we opt to focus on party evaluations here.

Table 2 Examples of open-ended responses to party evaluation questions, 2020 ANES

Democratic Party Likes: Is there anything you like about the Democratic Party?
- "They support better healthcare coverage for more people, want to combat climate change, support science-based measures to fight the pandemic, do not want to limit access to contraception or abortion, and are more willing to work towards equality regardless of race, sex, sexual orientation, etc. Their economic policies are more supportive of middle- and lower-income people, rather than just helping the rich get richer."
- "They actually care about Americans and providing adequate health care and education. They support a woman's right to choose what is right for her body."
- "Commitment to abortion rights."

Democratic Party Dislikes: Is there anything you dislike about the Democratic Party?
- "The only thing I do not like about the Democratic Party is its stance on abortion. While I feel like in certain circumstances, abortion is an acceptable choice, I do not believe that it is in every circumstance. I do believe that a woman should have the right to choose over her own body, but when there is a heartbeat in the baby inside her, I believe that makes that baby a person and takes her right to choose if that baby should live or die away from her except for certain circumstances."
- "Race baiting tactics, Women's right to choose, Anti-police."
- "They back abortion all the way up to the day the baby is born. They are for socialism. They want to raise taxes. The Democrats let the cities of Portland and Seattle be very nearly destroyed and would not let Trump send anyone in to stop the destruction. This is obscene! Pelosi? She is horrible and goes against everything I stand for."

Republican Party Likes: Is there anything you like about the Republican Party?
- "High moral ground, focus on small business America and the people, pro-life policies, the belief in small federal government control, freedom of choice for healthcare, education, among other things."
- "Patriotic. Pro-space exploration. Supports small businesses. Desires to bring business back to the U.S. Protects borders. Vigilant about who enters our country. Pro-life."
- "They want less government control. They want lower taxes. They want to repeal *Roe v. Wade*."

Table 2 (cont.)

Republican Party Dislikes: Is there anything you dislike about the Republican Party?
- "They support a pro-life policy but then do not support the very children and mothers who result from these policies (through their constant assault on food stamps, child care benefits, and birth control/healthcare benefits). They use their religious views to drive policy decisions. They support widespread and dangerous gun policies that result in the needless death of thousands of Americans."
- "They are pro-life and I support pro-choice!"
- "Many of their policies are not inclusive nor are they a way for people to advance from their current stations. Many policies are contrary, but the biggest one for me is the constant battle for pro-life legislation while not supporting policies like welfare to support the people who they are forcing into family situations."

respondents whose comments were included in Table 2, are classified as abortion-focused Americans.

Coding Strategy

Our approach to identifying abortion-focused Americans combined automated and human coding. Initially, we used automated text analysis to identify open-ended survey responses that mentioned abortion. Based on our knowledge of the issue, we constructed a list of keywords and phrases that might reflect mentions of abortion or reproductive rights. These keywords consisted of terms like abortion, choice, life, unborn, and fetus. (See Table A1 Appendix A for the complete dictionary.)[35] We erred on the side of creating an expansive list, recognizing that it was preferable to flag responses for human coding that did not discuss abortion compared to missing responses that did discuss abortion in our initial draw of the data.[36]

Of the approximately 20,700 people surveyed across election years, 81 percent answered at least one of the party evaluation questions.[37] Coders evaluated 4,853 of

---
[35] When the survey was administered using a computer-assisted mode, the answers to the party likes and dislikes questions were entered by the respondent. In other interview modes (i.e., phone or face-to-face), an interviewer would have recorded the responses. The data entry and transcription process introduces potential for error. All responses were cleaned to eliminate spelling mistakes to increase the accuracy of our dictionary-based approach.
[36] For information about the coverage check we performed on our dictionary, see the note accompanying Table A1 in Appendix A.
[37] Survey respondents who answered these questions were not broadly representative of the American public. They had significantly higher levels of political knowledge and interest than those who opted not to answer. They were also more likely to be college-educated. Thus, the answers analyzed here are drawn from a more highly engaged subset of the American electorate. For more details about these survey respondents, please see Table A3 and Figure A1 in Appendix A.

these open-ended responses flagged by our dictionary and determined 4,064 were relevant (e.g., making, at minimum, a vague reference to choice or life, or including a reference to women's rights generally), and 3,220 explicitly referenced abortion. We took a conservative definition of explicit mentions, for example, coding "reproductive rights" as an explicit mention but not something like "status of women," which is a broader category that may or may not be intended to include abortion rights. Respondents whose party evaluations included at least one explicit reference to abortion were classified as abortion-focused Americans. In total, 2,389 unique respondents (or 11.5 percent of the sample) made an explicit reference to abortion.[38] The proportion varies somewhat from year-to-year, rising slightly from 10.4 in 2008 to 11.9 in 2012, then dipping to 8.1 percent in 2016. Abortion mentions increase to 14.2 percent of the sample in 2020, likely in response to the heightened salience of abortion sparked by Amy Coney Barrett's appointment to the Supreme Court just prior to the election.

In spite of the limitations of importance measures for distinguishing among issue priorities, we would expect there to be some relationship between importance ratings for abortion and the likelihood of mentioning it in the party evaluations. As noted prior, only the 2020 ANES included a question that asked "How important is this issue to you personally?"[39] Responses were given on a 5-point scale ranging from not at all important to extremely important. Overall, 80.3 percent of people who mentioned abortion in the open-ended evaluations said abortion is "very" or "extremely important" compared to 50.4 percent of people who did not mention abortion – a difference of 29.9 percentage points. While importance measures are perhaps imperfect proxies for preference intensity, given that they tend to be inflated, the difference in average importance scores suggests our approach is capturing a meaningful difference between Americans we classified as abortion-focused and those we did not.

We also considered the relationship between abortion focus and issue importance across party lines. The results are depicted in Figure 7. Regardless of party identification, abortion-focused Americans rated abortion as a more important issue compared to their counterparts with less intense abortion preferences. In each case, the difference between partisans with and without abortion focus is statistically significant.[40] Abortion-focused partisans were nearly twice as

---

[38] The difference between the number of explicit abortion mentions (3,220) and the number of abortion-focused respondents (2,389) occurs because some respondents made multiple mentions of abortion across the four party evaluation questions.

[39] This question immediately followed the standard issue position question for abortion, which is why it does not include the word "abortion."

[40] Information about the statistical significance of the differences presented in Figure 5.1 is as follows: Democrats: $F(1,8835)=111.08$, $p<.001$; independents: $F(1,8835)=36.10$, $p<.001$; Republicans: $F(1,8835) = 263.53$, $p<.001$.

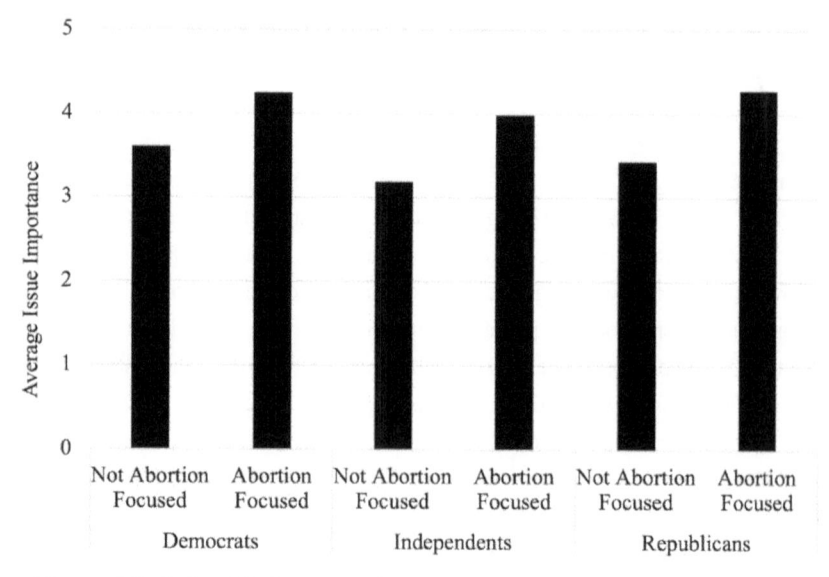

Figure 7 Relationship between abortion focus and issue importance, 2020

likely to rate the issue as "extremely important." Consistent with our expectations, these comparisons reveal that abortion importance is much greater among abortion-focused Americans regardless of their partisan affiliation.

Who Are the Abortion-Focused Americans?

Abortion-focused Americans have a few things in common. For instance, they are twice as likely to identify with the Republican Party. Across the four elections we examined, 8.4 percent of Democrats were categorized as abortion-focused compared to 16.8 percent of Republicans. They also share certain demographic characteristics. For instance, 17.0 percent of Americans with a college degree were classified as abortion-focused, compared to 9.6 percent of Americans without a college degree. About 56 percent of abortion-focused Americans were women. Evangelical identification was more common among Americans with intense abortion preferences compared to those with weaker preferences, and people in this group report more frequent church attendance as well.[41]

The higher concentration of abortion-focused Republicans is consistent with our arguments about the greater centrality of abortion to the Republican Party's electoral strategy relative to that of the Democratic Party. Disaggregating abortion mentions into likes and dislikes based on partisanship is also

---

[41] See Figure A2 in Appendix A for more information about correlates of abortion focus.

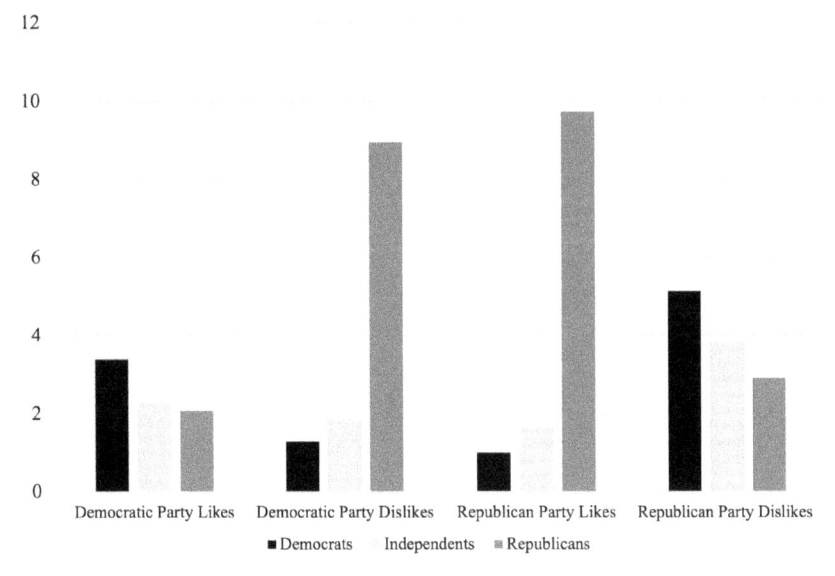

Abortion Attitudes and Polarization in the American Electorate 51

Figure 8 Abortion mentions in party likes and dislikes, 2008–2020 pooled

instructive, see Figure 8. Republicans – who mention abortion most frequently – tend to do so primarily in two circumstances: when describing things they like about their own party and when describing things they dislike about the Democratic Party. By contrast, Democrats and independents are much more likely to mention abortion when describing something they dislike about the Republican Party. But, they do so with considerably less frequency. The asymmetry suggests abortion may be more central to Republicans' conceptualization of partisanship.

To get a sense of how demographic factors intersect with partisanship to shape abortion focus, we estimated a series of logit models predicting whether or not Democrats, independents, and Republicans mentioned abortion in their party evaluations. The factors shaping abortion focus are depicted in Figure 9. Each variable is coded so that the minimum value is zero and the maximum value is one, and the plot includes the estimated coefficient along with a 95 percent confidence interval. Coefficients with confidence intervals that do not overlap the vertical line at zero are significantly related to abortion focus.[42]

Some of these demographic factors have consistent effects across partisanship. For instance, women in both the Democratic and Republican Party are more

---
[42] Survey weights are applied. Election year fixed effects were included in the model but are not depicted. For more information about how variables were constructed for this model and the estimation strategy, see Tables A4 and A5 in Appendix A.

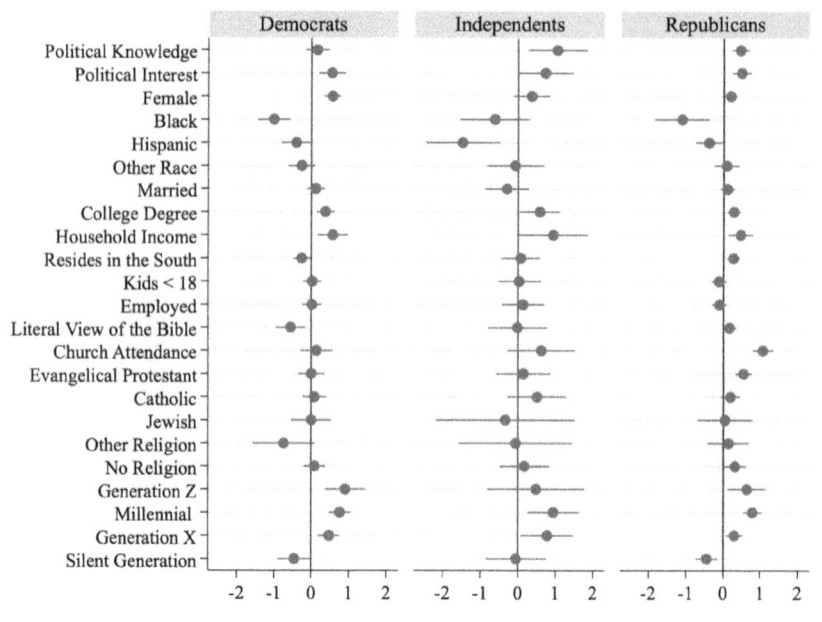

Figure 9 Predictors of abortion focus, 2008–2020 pooled

likely to be categorized as abortion-focused compared to men. Political interest is positively associated with abortion focus for both parties, as are income and having completed a four-year college degree. Younger Americans are more likely to be abortion focused, whereas Black Americans are less likely to be classified as abortion focused, regardless of party. Other factors that contribute to abortion focus are contingent on partisanship. Political knowledge is linked abortion focus for independents and Republicans, but not Democrats. Indicators of religiosity – namely frequency of church attendance and evangelical identification – boost abortion focus in Republicans but not Democrats or independents. This result is consistent with the notion that evangelical Protestants are an important part of the Republican coalition with intense preferences about abortion, a point outlined in greater detail back in Section 1.

Thematic Analysis of Abortion Mentions in the Party Evaluation Questions

The answers people gave to the party evaluation questions can tell us more still about abortion attitudes if we consider not only *whether* abortion was mentioned, but also *how* it was mentioned. When answering these questions, some people mentioned abortion only briefly, and the word "abortion" or "pro-life" or "pro-choice" was the sum total of their response. But others elaborated on the issue, linking their position on abortion to their values, women's rights, or the courts, among other factors. These more elaborated responses provide a window into what Americans with intense issue preferences want when it comes to abortion policy. In this section, we report the results from a more detailed coding of the themes and issues mentioned alongside abortion to better understand intense abortion preferences and how they fit into the bigger picture of a polarized American electorate.

Recall, our research assistants evaluated all survey responses flagged by our dictionary to verify whether each was, in fact, a clear reference to abortion. These assistants also evaluated the broader content of each survey response and indicated the presence of related concepts reflecting salient dimensions of the abortion debate, namely: qualified support for abortion, women's rights, family values, ideology, religion, other issues, and judges and courts.[43] In Table 3, we offer examples of the major themes from the 2020 survey to provide a sense of how they typically showed up in party evaluations.

How commonplace were these themes? In Table 4 we document their prevalence among abortion-focused Americans in the ANES surveys between 2008 and 2020.[44] The figures are divided by party to highlight areas of commonality and difference between Democrats and Republicans.[45] A key takeaway from these data is that most abortion-focused Americans mention at least one issue other than abortion. Republicans are somewhat more likely to only mention abortion, but the overwhelming majority (73.5 percent) mention a second issue in addition to abortion. This result is somewhat contrary to the popular notion that people with intense preferences about abortion might be "single-issue" voters for whom abortion is their primary (or only) concern when it comes to electoral politics. Instead, our findings suggest abortion is connected with a constellation of other issue attitudes as well as to the parties themselves. This observation brings to mind Layman and Carsey's (1998) theory of conflict extension, which posits that conflict between the parties has expanded from a single dimension focused on moral or economic issues to encompass a broad

---

[43] The coding criteria are provided in Table A2 of Appendix A.
[44] Because the data are drawn only from the subset of respondents who answered the open-ended questions and mentioned abortion, the data are not weighted to population benchmarks.
[45] Our analysis suggests that partisanship is the major dividing line among Americans when it comes to abortion attitudes. We also evaluated gender differences in themes and did not uncover many. Women were significantly more likely to mention women's rights compared to men (28 percent compared to 18 percent, p<.001) and significantly less likely to mention another issue alongside abortion (75 percent compared to 80 percent, p>.001), though this difference is relatively modest.

Table 3 Examples of themes from manual coding of the open-ended party evaluations

Theme	Examples
Qualified Support	"I feel like they need to be more involved with the living people of the USA. Yes they can help but they can also overdo it, such as **an abortion in extremely early stages or extreme cases is ok but abortion on a baby who would be able to survive outside the womb is not ok**." [Republican Party Dislikes]
Women's Rights	"Bunch of old white men looking out for themselves. I am for the right to abortion, and **women's rights** in general. I am in favor of a single payer health care system." [Republican Party Dislikes]
Family Values	"Stand for the Constitution, second amendment, lower taxes, **family values** and anti-abortion." [Republican Party Likes]
Ideology	"**Liberalism** in areas of gender; late term abortion rights; its **lean toward socialism**" [Democratic Party Dislikes]
Religion	"pro-choice, defund the police, **inconsistencies with biblical teaching**, unorganized, scornful." [Democratic Party Dislikes]
Other Issues	"They support **lowering taxes**, **free market capitalism**, restrictions on **immigration**, increased **military spending**, **gun rights**, restrictions on abortion, **deregulation** and **restrictions on labor unions**." [Republican Party Likes]
Judges and Courts	"Anti-immigration, anti-gay and transgender, anti-Medicare, anti-environment, will say or do anything to enrich their financial backers, anti-abortion and women's rights, anti-regulation, **stacking the courts with conservative judges**, racist." [Republican Party Dislikes]

<u>Note</u>: These responses are lightly edited for grammar and/or brevity. Some answers may have been coded for multiple themes; we have only highlighted the theme linked to the specified category.

Table 4 Related themes among abortion mentioners, 2008–2020 pooled

	Democrats	Independents	Republicans	Dem–Rep Difference
Other Issues	82.94	72.15	73.49	9.45***
Women's Rights	43.96	28.57	8.13	35.83***
Religion	20.36	18.28	18.65	1.71
Ideology	18.36	16.67	27.58	−9.22***
Family Values	8.05	9.42	8.73	−0.68
Judges and Courts	4.19	2.25	1.9	2.29**
Qualified Support	2.55	3.37	3.87	−1.32

Note: Entries are percentages. The difference column is a test of proportions comparing Democrats and Republicans. *p<.05, **p<.01, ***p<.001.

range of political issues spanning moral, economic, and other considerations (see also Bawn et al. 2012).

As one might expect, Democrats were significantly more likely than Republicans to discuss abortion using a "women's rights" frame (about 44 percent compared to 8 percent).[46] For example, one Democratic survey respondent described something they disliked about the Republican Party this way: "I am for the right to abortion, and **women's rights** in general." A Republican survey respondent described something they disliked about the Democratic Party this way: "They are in favor of **murdering babies under the pretext of women's rights**." Both people invoked the same theme, though the first case reflects an endorsement of framing abortion in terms of women's rights, whereas the second example reflects a rejection of that frame.

Republicans were more likely to include references to ideology when speaking about abortion compared to Democrats (27.6 percent compared to 18.4 percent). These references typically characterized the opposition's viewpoints as outside the mainstream. An example from Table 3 illustrates this point. In it, a Republican described something they disliked about the Democratic Party in ideological terms: "**Liberalism** in areas of gender; late term abortion rights; its **lean toward socialism**."

There were some points of commonality in our analysis as well. For instance, Democrats and Republicans were about equally likely to mention family values and religion in their party evaluations though, as was the case in the "women's

---
[46] Recall from Section 2 that references to things like "the status of women" that did not expressly mention abortion were not counted as abortion mentions. This may result in an undercount among Democrats for this category.

rights" example previously, partisans tended to invoke these concepts in somewhat different ways. Democrats and Republicans also mentioned qualified support for abortion – suggesting it should be legal in some circumstances and illegal in others – in similar proportions.

Conclusion

The analysis presented here suggests our approach to identifying abortion-focused Americans from the open-ended party evaluations captures a subset of the public who share intense preferences. Regardless of the positions they take on the issue, this group relies more heavily on abortion when thinking about party politics. We gained a few key insights about abortion focus as well – namely, that it is more common in the Republican Party and that abortion-focused Americans are not likely to be "single issue" voters. In addition, our results suggest the proportion of abortion-focused Americans is not fixed over time. The public responds to changes in the salience of the issue, likely to threats and opportunities related to policy at the federal and state levels. This is a point we will return to in our final chapter.

Our thematic analysis offered some preliminary insights into the preferences of abortion-focused Americans as well as some important points of commonality and difference across the parties. In the coming section, we make some structured comparisons between Americans with high and low preference intensity in order to better understand the role abortion-focused Americans play in electoral politics and the influence they exert on policy. The results suggest that preference intensity is associated with higher rates of political engagement – or behavioral polarization – as intensity theory suggests. But, it is associated with other manifestations of polarization as well, suggesting that ongoing conflict over abortion rights may serve to bolster partisan polarization in the future.

6 Abortion Focus and Polarization

In Section 4, we demonstrated that abortion attitudes have become more polarized along party lines over time. This is part of a growing trend toward an era of heightened partisan division, wherein partisanship is increasingly determinative of a host of political opinions and behaviors. Now that we have laid the groundwork for measuring preference intensity, we can dig deeper into the role it plays in polarization in the electorate and the likely influence it will have on future elections, given the ongoing and salient conflict over abortion rights. Intensity theory suggests that small constituencies with intense preferences have a disproportionate impact on policy by creating electoral incentives for representation based on their high and sustained levels of participation (Bishin

2009; Hill 2022; Iyengar and Krupenkin 2018). In this respect, elites are responsive to constituencies that are behaviorally polarized (comparatively more politically active) compared with larger constituencies with less intense preferences. Prior research into the psychology of political mobilization indicates strong affective (or emotional) reactions to politics often underlie political behavior, suggesting behavioral polarization and affective polarization are intertwined processes (Huddy et al. 2015; Valentino et al. 2011). Beyond this, we consider a third manifestation of polarization – preference extremity, also known as issue-based or attitudinal polarization.

In the analysis that follows, we uncover evidence that intense preferences about abortion rights are related to all three of these forms of polarization. Abortion-focused Americans in both parties hold significantly more absolutist preferences about abortion rights (i.e., preferring abortion always be legal or always be illegal) compared to Americans with less intense preferences, who tend to report more situationist viewpoints (i.e., preferring abortion be legal in some cases, illegal in others). Abortion focus is associated with stronger emotional reactions to the parties and to proposed changes in abortion rights, as well as higher rates of electoral participation. Our findings are consistent with expectations derived from intensity theory. The attitudinal and behavioral correlates of preference intensity suggest that intense minorities send more extreme and consistent signals about their preferences to elected officials and, as a result, may disproportionately influence policy.

Are Abortion-Focused Americans More Participatory?

Mobilization is critical to intensity theory. Because preference intensity is difficult for leaders to discern, they must rely on signals from the electorate to infer the scope and intensity of the public's commitment to a particular policy outcome (Hill 2022). Voters with intense preferences are more willing to bear the costs associated with participation in order to communicate their desires to elected officials. Their higher levels of participation – also known as behavioral polarization – can show up in a number of ways, from involvement in campaigns and elections (e.g., voting or volunteering for a candidate or party), to commitment of financial support (e.g., donating to candidates, parties, and PACs), as well as a tendency to discuss politics more frequently with friends and family (e.g., Abramowitz 2010; Mason 2018). We consider a few of these activities in this section.

First, rates of voter turnout by abortion focus and partisanship are provided in Figure 10. Abortion-focused Democrats, independents, and Republicans all turn out at significantly higher rates than other Americans.[47] The difference is especially

---

[47] Comparisons were made using Adjusted Wald tests: Democrats $F(1,18,841)=29.93$, $p<.001$; independents $F(1, 18,841)=23.90$, $p<.001$; Republicans $F(1, 18,841)=52.88$, $p<.001$.

58   *Gender and Politics*

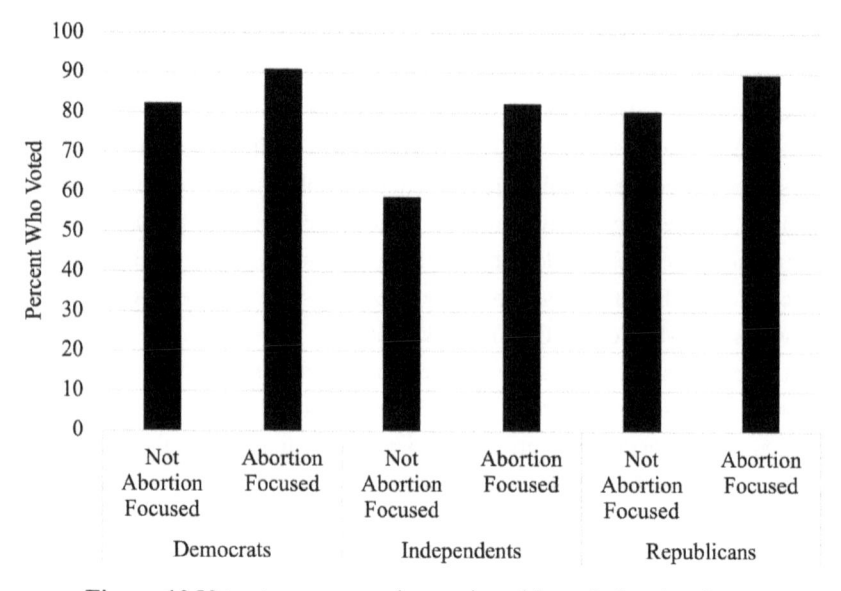

Figure 10 Voter turnout rates by partisanship and abortion focus, 2008–2020 pooled

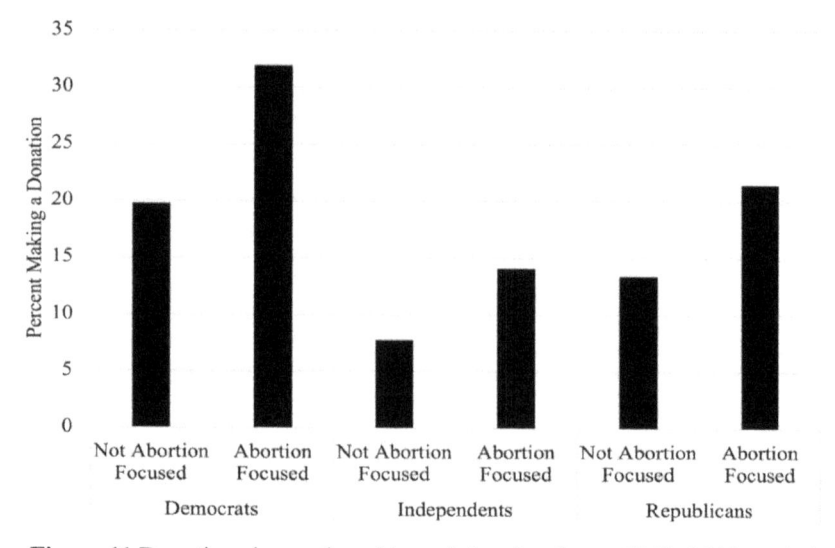

Figure 11 Donations by partisanship and abortion focus, 2008–2020 pooled

pronounced among independents, though this group is quite small. There is a 23.6 point difference in turnout between abortion-focused independents and other independent identifiers. Differences among Democrats (8.6 points) and Republicans (9.3 points) are more modest by comparison, though still substantively meaningful, as electoral participation is an important currency for intense minorities. A similar pattern of results is evident for campaign donations. Figure 11

Abortion Attitudes and Polarization in the American Electorate 59

shows the percentage of people who donated to either a candidate, a political party, or some other political group based on partisanship and preference intensity. Regardless of partisanship, abortion focus is associated with higher rates of political donations and the differences among Democrats and Republicans based on abortion focus are statistically significant.[48]

We also consider the frequency with which abortion-focused Americans engage in political discussion with their peers. Prior research has established that the number of days spent discussing politics is an indicator of campaign engagement (see, for example, Campbell and Wolbrecht 2006; Hansen 1997). Survey respondents were asked how many days in the past week they discussed politics with family or friends. Responses ranged from zero to seven days. Average rates of discussion are depicted in Figure 12. In each case, discussion frequency was significantly higher among abortion-focused partisans.[49] Once again, the difference was largest among independents, with abortion-focused independents reporting about 0.58 days more of political discussion compared to somewhat more moderate differences among Democrats (0.37 days difference) and Republicans (0.49 days difference).

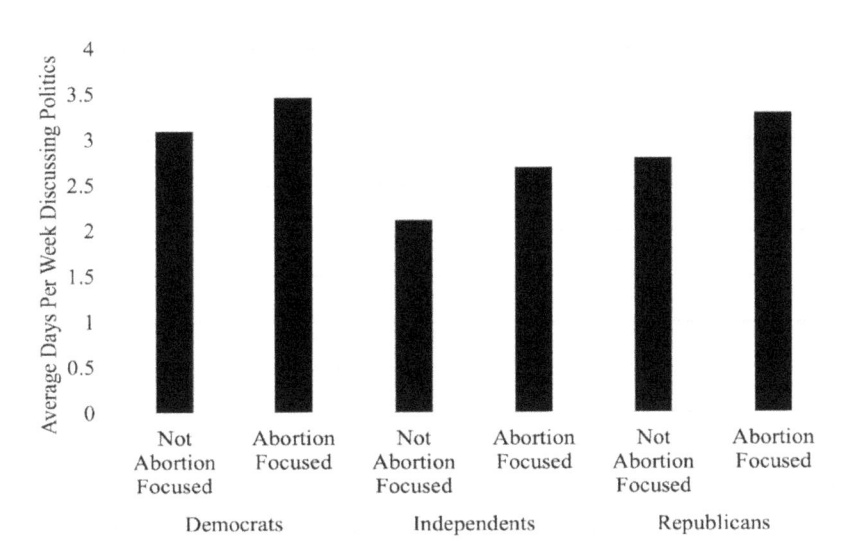

Figure 12 Political discussion frequency by partisanship and abortion focus, 2008–2020 pooled

---

[48] Statistical significance was gauged by Adjusted Wald Tests – for Democrats: $F(1,19201) = 29.09$, $p<.001$ and for Republicans $F(1,19201) = 26.42$, $p<.001$. While abortion-focused independents donate at higher rates than other independents, the difference is only marginally significant [$F(1,19201) = 3.54$, $p=.06$].

[49] Comparisons were made using Adjusted Wald tests: Democrats: $F(1, 19192)=9.42$, $p<.01$; independents: $F(1, 19192)=7.38$, $p<.01$; Republicans: $F(1, 19192)=29.97$, $p<.001$.

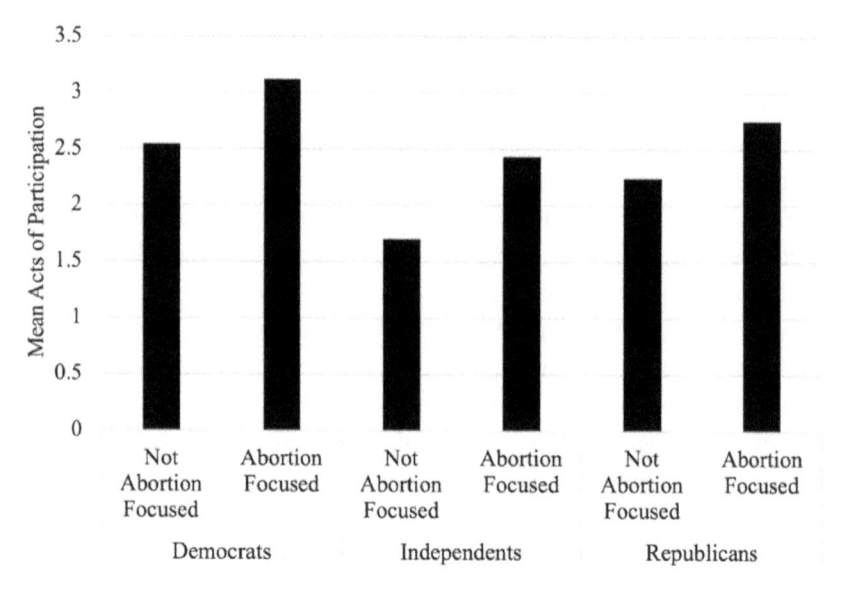

Figure 13 Overall participation rates by partisanship and abortion focus, 2008–2020 pooled

Our last look at behavioral polarization evaluates overall levels of involvement in campaigns, measured as a count of ten self-reported activities, including: voting, attending meetings, displaying campaign materials, other campaign work, donating to a candidate, party or related group, discussing politics with another person, attending a political protest, or contacting a member of Congress. As Figure 13 shows, mean participation rates across groups were significantly different based on abortion focus.[50] Substantively, mean differences amounted to about half an act of political participation for Democrats (0.58) and Republicans (0.51) and about three-quarters of an act for independents (0.74).

Across our four indicators of participation, we find consistent evidence that Americans who think abortion is a salient and important criterion for evaluating the parties participate at higher rates. Mean rates of participation for abortion-focused partisans hover around three acts of participation in an election year, consistent with an established standard for "occasional activists" in the electorate (e.g., Carmines and Woods 2002). Though we observed roughly equivalent rates of behavioral polarization across party lines, it is important to keep in mind there are more abortion-focused Republicans, so the comparable rates of participation observed here do not necessarily translate into comparable influence in the aggregate. Instead, the greater proportion of abortion-focused

---

[50] Comparisons were made using Adjusted Wald tests: Democrats: $F(1,18752)=40.26$, $p<.001$; independents: $F(1, 18752)=25.23$, $p<.001$; Republicans: $F(1, 18752)=67.72$, $p<.001$.

Republicans likely drives the outsized influence of this intense and active minority. These results conform to expectations stemming from intensity theory, which posits that preference intensity is linked to broader engagement in electoral politics as well as willingness to engage in costly forms of political participation in exchange for policy influence.

Are Abortion-Focused Americans More Affectively Polarized?

Intensity theory does not specify a role for emotion in the link between preference intensity and participation. Yet, political psychology research suggests emotion and mobilization typically go hand-in-hand. Political conflict often invokes threats to identity and moral convictions, and this is certainly the case for abortion rights. Intense political conflict can elicit strong emotions and stir people with deeply held identities and preferences to action (Enders and Lupton 2021; Huddy et al. 2015; Martel et al. 2021). This might involve emotional reactions to the issue itself (i.e., changes in policy that are proposed or accomplished) or more generalized emotional reactions toward the parties and political system. Abortion attitudes have been identified as a distinctive driver of a phenomenon referred to as affective polarization – the growing divide between the positive feelings (or affect) people hold for their party and the negative feelings they hold toward the opposition party (Ondercin and Lizotte 2021). Next, we explore the link between preference intensity and affective polarization.

The ANES has not historically included measures of emotions linked directly to the abortion debate. However, given the growing salience of the issue, one such question was included in the 2020 survey. It asked, "Would you be pleased, upset, or neither pleased nor upset if the Supreme Court reduced abortion rights?" and followed up with a question about intensity, resulting in a 7-point Likert scale ranging from (1) extremely pleased to (7) extremely upset. Responses are presented in Figure 14, and the pattern of results suggests preference intensity corresponds to greater emotional investment in the issue. Abortion-focused Democrats were significantly more upset about the prospect of the Supreme Court restricting abortion rights than were other Democrats. And, abortion-focused Republicans were significantly more pleased about this prospect compared to other members of their party.[51] Differences based on abortion focus were substantially greater among Republicans however – a 1.2 difference on the 7-point scale compared to only a 0.48 point difference among Democrats.

---

[51] Comparisons were made using Adjusted Wald tests: Democrats: $F(1,8803)=19.31$, $p<.001$; independents: $F(1, 8803)=2.78$, $p=.10$; Republicans: $F(1,8803)=152.29$, $p<.001$.

Figure 14 Emotional reactions to changing abortion rights, 2020

A second way that affective polarization manifests is in terms of the growing divide between how Americans evaluate their own party and how they view members of the opposition party. This concept is sometimes referred to as *warmth bias* because evaluations are measured on a metric known as a feeling thermometer (Mason 2018). Feeling thermometers ask people to rate a candidate, group, or party on a scale ranging from zero to 100, where zero reflects a very negative rating, 100 represents a very positive rating, and 50 represents a neutral rating. To determine warmth bias in a partisan context, researchers calculate the absolute difference in the rating of the Democratic Party and the rating of the Republican Party. As the absolute difference between the two evaluations grows, so does the extent of warmth bias.

Warmth bias is depicted in Figure 15. There is about a 50-point difference in the ratings Democrats provide for their own party and the Republican Party regardless of whether they are classified as abortion-focused. By contrast, warmth bias is significantly greater among independents and Republicans who are abortion-focused.[52] On average, abortion-focused independents have a greater warmth bias of about 7.4 points. Similarly, abortion-focused Republicans have a warmth bias about 7.8 points greater than their non-abortion-focused Republican counterparts. These findings provide some support for the idea that abortion focus is associated with affective polarization,

---

[52] Comparisons based on abortion focus within each group were conducted via Adjusted Wald tests: Democrats: $F(1, 20317)=0.07$, n.s; independents: $F(1, 20317)=11.15$, $p<.001$; Republicans $F(1, 20317)=48.39$, $p<.001$.

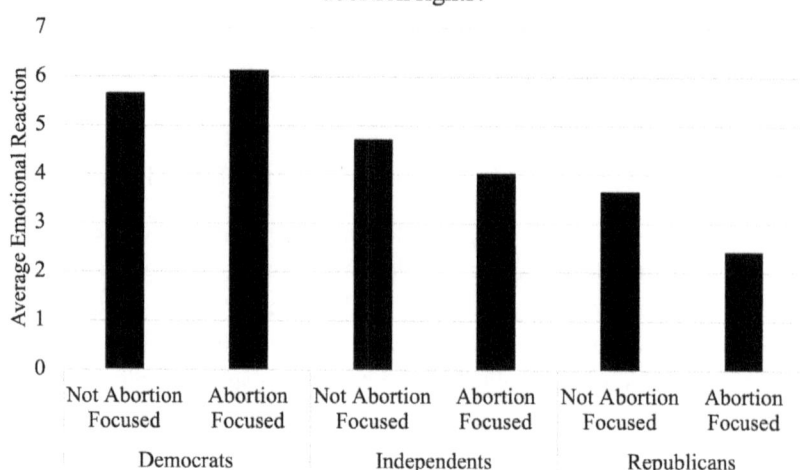

Abortion Attitudes and Polarization in the American Electorate

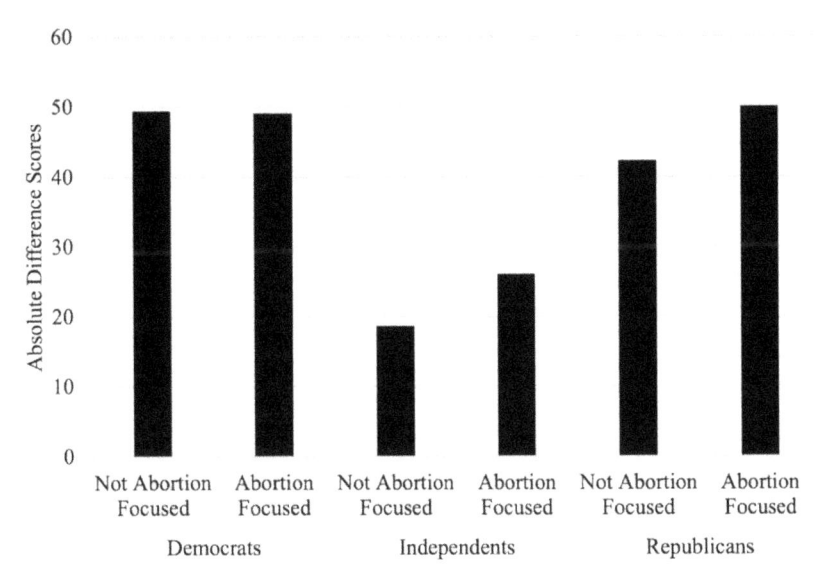

Figure 15 Party thermometer ratings, 2008–2020 pooled
Note: Entries are average absolute differences in thermometer ratings. Survey weights are applied.

though the pattern of results is more consistent for Republicans. Democrats, by contrast, report high levels of affective polarization regardless of their preference intensity on abortion rights. This party asymmetry suggests abortion focus is more central to evaluations of the parties among Republicans compared to Democrats.[53]

This analysis suggests that preference intensity is associated with affective polarization in addition to behavioral polarization. We will revisit this point in Section 7, when we explore emotional reactions to the *Dobbs* decision and political mobilization stemming from concern over abortion in the 2022 midterm elections. But first, we turn to a final manifestation of polarization and consider whether preference intensity is linked to preference extremity when it comes to abortion rights.

Do Abortion-Focused Americans Have More Extreme Preferences?

To evaluate whether the preferences of abortion-focused Americans are distinct and more extreme when compared to other Americans, we revisit the survey question that asked respondents to select one of the following four statements that best describes their view: (1) by law, abortion should never be permitted, (2)

---

[53] We also uncovered modest evidence of affective polarization in the candidate thermometer ratings. See Figure A3 in the Online Appendix for details.

the law should permit abortion only in case of rape, incest, or when the woman's life is in danger, (3) the law should permit abortion other than for rape/incest/danger to a woman but only after the need clearly established, and (4) by law, a woman should always be able to obtain an abortion as a matter of personal choice. Responses are provided Table 5 and presented based on party identification and abortion focus.

The distribution of responses to the question differs significantly based on abortion focus for each of the three groups. Among abortion-focused Democrats, 78.4 percent said abortion should always be permitted, compared to 63.2 percent of Democrats who were not classified as abortion-focused. A similar pattern is evident for independents: abortion focus is associated with a greater tendency to support abortion rights. Republicans, however, are a bit more divided on the issue. There is a clear difference between abortion-focused Republicans and their counterparts in the two most extreme categories. Abortion-focused Republicans are more than twice as likely to take a position that abortion should never be permitted (36.5 percent compared to 15.6 percent). Unsurprisingly, they are also much less likely to indicate that abortion should always be permitted (16.6 percent compared to 30.1 percent for Americans less focused on abortion).

For both groups of Republicans, the modal response was that abortion should be permitted in a narrow set of cases, specifically: "the law should permit abortion only in case of rape, incest, or when the woman's life is in danger." In these kinds of cases, a woman's decision to have an abortion is driven largely by circumstances beyond her control. Thus, while abortion focus reflects a difference of opinion among Republicans, it is clear that the Republican Party is more internally divided on this issue compared to abortion-focused Democrats and even independents.

Though the parties differ in this respect, it is clear that for both Democrats and Republicans, intense preferences are related to more extreme positions on abortion. Abortion-focused partisans were more likely to select absolutist positions (i.e., abortion should always be legal or never be legal) compared to their counterparts with less intense preferences who more commonly selected situational factors (e.g., abortion should be legal in some, but not all, cases).

To gain more insight into how people evaluate the circumstances surrounding abortion decision-making, we turn to a series of more targeted questions from the 2008 and 2012 ANES surveys that focus on discrete situational factors.[54] These questions were not asked in the 2016 or 2020 ANES surveys. Though

---

[54] In 2008, these questions were posed to a random sample of half of the ANES respondents. The question asking about abortion "for any reason" was asked only in 2012.

Table 5 Relationship between abortion focus and issue positions, 2008–2020 pooled

	Democrats		Independents		Republicans	
	Not Abortion-focused	Abortion-focused	Not Abortion-focused	Abortion-focused	Not Abortion-focused	Abortion-focused
Never Permitted	6.71	5.06	9.24	6.63	15.56	36.48
Narrow Set of Cases	16.59	9.08	22.87	20.43	37.72	37.57
Broader Set of Cases	13.49	7.47	16.89	10.51	16.66	9.40
Always Permitted	63.20	78.38	51.00	62.43	30.06	16.55
	$\chi^2(3) = 70.81, p < .001$		$\chi^2(3) = 9.76, p = .14$		$\chi^2(3) = 368.98, p < .001$	

Note: Entries are percentages. Survey weights are applied.

admittedly these data are a bit dated, survey items asking about the specific circumstances surrounding abortion are useful in the current policy landscape, as many state legislatures are now in the process of pursuing new laws that reconsider the various circumstances surrounding abortion and many courts are evaluating the legality of exemptions tied to these circumstances.

Unlike the standard abortion opinion question, which lumps together several circumstances ("the law should permit abortion only in case of rape, incest, or when the woman's life is in danger" and "the law should permit abortion other than for rape/incest/danger to a woman but only after the need is clearly established"), this approach asks about individual circumstances in isolation and does not rely on individual interpretations of ambiguous language like "clearly established need." In these questions, participants were asked about their support for abortion in eight specific scenarios including: when the mother faced a fatal health risk, when the mother faced a nonfatal health risk, when the pregnancy resulted from rape, when the pregnancy resulted from incest, in the case of a fetal defect, when the family faced financial hardship, because the parents wished to choose the gender of the baby, and lastly, for any reason at all.

The eight circumstances reflect a fairly comprehensive list, consisting of reasons widely considered to be circumstances out of a woman's control (e.g., sexual violence and health risk to the mother and or fetus), and areas more closely tied to women's reproductive discretion (e.g., financial reasons, gender selection, or any reason). When posed with each of these discrete circumstances, survey participants selected a response on a scale ranging from (1) oppose a great deal to (9) favor a great deal.[55] In Table 6, we compare responses to these questions among partisans based on whether they were classified as abortion-focused. The table contains average scores on each item and the absolute difference between these two groups with a notation indicating whether the differences are statistically significant.

Among Democrats, it is clear that those with intense preferences about abortion were significantly more supportive of abortion rights across the full range of circumstances, which is consistent with our expectations about preference intensity and issue extremity. Yet, there was some variation. For instance, overall support was still quite low in cases where abortion is performed because a person wishes to select the sex of their baby, regardless of abortion focus. And abortion-focused Democrats were not unanimous in their support for abortion when it stems from financial hardship.

---

[55] The original scale ran in the opposite direction. We reverse-coded responses to these items to provide a more intuitive interpretation, with higher scores corresponding to higher levels of support.

Table 6 Support for abortion in specific circumstances, 2008 and 2012 only

	Democrats			Independents			Republicans		
	Not Abortion-focused	Abortion-focused	|Diff|	Not Abortion-focused	Abortion-focused	|Diff|	Not Abortion-focused	Abortion-focused	|Diff|
Fatal Risk	7.64	8.42	0.78***	7.91	8.58	0.67***	7.25	6.43	0.82***
Nonfatal Risk	5.99	7.36	1.37***	6.08	7.41	1.33***	4.94	3.78	1.16***
Incest	6.17	7.62	1.45***	6.34	8.00	1.66***	5.37	4.17	1.20***
Rape	7.54	8.36	0.82***	7.84	8.22	0.38	6.78	5.14	1.64***
Fetal Defect	6.41	7.31	0.90***	6.69	7.16	0.47	5.49	3.98	1.51***
Financial	4.56	5.87	1.31***	4.38	5.74	1.36**	3.13	2.47	0.66***
Select Sex	2.37	3.14	0.77**	2.25	3.49	1.24**	1.84	1.67	0.17
Any Reason	5.76	7.51	1.75***	6.03	7.33	1.30***	4.03	2.97	1.06***

Note: Entries are mean values on 9-point Likert scales. The *Diff* columns are the absolute difference between the average rating of abortion-focused and not abortion-focused survey respondents. Significance tests associated with group differences are denoted *p<.05, **p<.01, ***p<.001. Survey weights are applied.

Here is a little added context about these two circumstances. First, it is unclear how common the practice of sex-selective abortion is in the United States. Research suggests it is more commonplace in countries with restrictive reproductive policies that limit the number of children people can have or in cultures with strong preferences for male offspring (for more information see Hesketh et al. 2011). The issue has emerged in American policy debates. As of August 2023, eleven states had policies in effect that prohibit abortion on the basis of sex, and members of Congress have repeatedly introduced legislation (i. e., the Prenatal Nondiscrimination Act) that would prohibit abortion based on the sex or race of the fetus (Guttmacher 2023).

Second, seeking an abortion for financial reasons seemed to divide Democrats regardless of their abortion focus. Average scores for supporting abortion for any reason were considerably higher than support for financial reasons specifically, suggesting that financial circumstances are not part of the calculus most Americans make when they think of the "any reason" category. According to "The TurnAway Study" conducted by researchers at the University of California, San Francisco, women who are denied abortion services and go on to give birth experience a range of negative socioeconomic consequences, including an increase in household poverty, an inability to cover basic living expenses, and higher levels of debt accumulation (Foster et al. 2022; Miller et al. 2023). Beyond this, the study suggests that women who were unable to obtain a wanted abortion had a three-times-greater likelihood of future unemployment compared to women who were able to obtain one (Foster et al. 2022). In addition to the financial consequences for women carrying unwanted pregnancies to term, one study found that children are more likely to be placed in the foster care system in states with restrictive abortion access. These children are more likely to face financial hardship throughout their lives (Adkins et al. 2024).

Recent data collected by PerryUndem, a nonpartisan public opinion research firm, suggest the public may have gained an improved understanding of the financial consequences of carrying an unwanted pregnancy to term in the decade since our data were collected. In a nationwide survey conducted in December 2021 and January 2022, researchers asked Americans about several potential outcomes when a woman who wants an abortion is unable to obtain one. A majority of survey participants highlighted financial difficulties as a key outcome. For example, 55 percent cited an increase in poverty and 68 percent cited greater reliance on government safety net programs as likely outcomes (PerryUndam 2022).

Returning to the public opinion data in Table 6, we gain further insights into the situational factors that divide Republicans on abortion. Support for abortion was fairly high among Republicans regardless of abortion focus when a woman faces a fatal health risk stemming from pregnancy or when a pregnancy results from rape. Republicans are also fairly uniform in their very low levels of support for legal abortion due to financial reasons or a desire to select the sex of their baby. The remaining circumstances divide abortion-focused Republicans from those with different issue priorities. In cases where a mother faces a nonfatal health risk, where there is a fetal defect, and when the pregnancy results from incest, the average abortion-focused Republican places themselves below the midpoint on the 9-point Likert scale (indicated opposition), and the average non-abortion-focused Republican places themself above the midpoint of the scale (indicating support). This pattern of results points to an intense minority dynamic operating within the Republican Party itself, with some of the party's most committed activists and policy demanders driving policy in an increasingly restrictive and absolutist direction. The data suggest that even for many abortion-focused Republicans, recent efforts to ban abortion – for instance, Idaho's recent efforts to ban and criminalize abortion procedures even in medical emergencies – do not align with their policy preferences.[56]

Aside from these insights into internal party dynamics, responses to these survey questions illustrate that abortion focus is linked to attitude polarization, such that abortion-focused Democrats are significantly more supportive of abortion across the range of rationales provided compared to Democrats who are not abortion-focused. And, abortion-focused Republicans are significantly less supportive of abortion across this same set of circumstances than Republicans who are not abortion-focused. In these respects, preference intensity is associated with more extreme and polarized preferences. At the same time, the results highlight some nuances in patterns of support, suggesting there is heterogeneity even among partisans for whom abortion is a salient and important issue. Collectively, these findings point to an important connection between preference intensity and polarization.

Conclusion

Abortion-focused Americans exhibit a variety of attitudes and behaviors associated with polarization. This group not only holds more absolutist preferences on abortion, which is indicative of issue-based or attitudinal polarization, but they also demonstrate more warmth bias when evaluating the parties and respond more strongly to the potential threat to the *Roe* precedent, a pattern indicative of affective polarization. Additionally, we find evidence that abortion-focused Americans are behaviorally polarized. They are more likely to vote, donate, discuss politics, and engage in other political activities, regardless

---

[56] For details, see Sherman (2023).

of their partisanship. The higher levels of issue-based, affective, and behavioral polarization observed among abortion-focused Americans is consistent with Hill's (2022) work on frustrated majorities, which implies that intense minorities will hold more extreme views and engage in more frequent and costly political action. The results presented here highlight the connection between issue attitudes, political identity, and polarization, illustrating the pathway of influence for intense minorities.

In the final section of this Element, we consider whether the *Dobbs* has meaningfully impacted these relationships. In the 2020 election, VanSickle-Ward and her colleagues (2023) found that women who were concerned that *Roe* might be overturned were motivated to turnout at higher rates. Evidence from the midterm elections in 2022 and elections in several key states in 2023 highlights the role of mobilization tied to abortion as well. An improved understanding of abortion-focused Americans is important moving forward, given the heightened salience of the abortion issue post-*Dobbs* and the likelihood of state-level ballot initiatives involving abortion in future elections. Next, we consider how preference intensity influenced electoral behavior in the 2022 midterm elections and conclude with a broader discussion of pathways to future policy congruence.

7 Electoral Politics Post-*Dobbs*

Our analysis in the previous section demonstrates that partisans with intense preferences about abortion rights hold more extreme issue positions, respond more emotionally to political threats, and engage more frequently in electoral politics in pursuit of their political goals, consistent with intensity theory. These sustained efforts, particularly among an intense minority of abortion-focused Americans in the Republican Party, gradually contributed to the *Dobbs* decision and the current abortion policy landscape in the United States more broadly. In this section, we turn to how the electoral dynamics of intense minorities of abortion-focused voters might shape the future of abortion rights.

Accounts of the 2022 midterms often spoke to a central role for abortion in mobilizing voters and shaping policy through direct ballot measures. Many of these developments were cast as victories for supporters of abortion rights, and framed as the successful mobilization of a frustrated majority of Americans in support of candidates and initiatives that would protect reproductive rights. The arguments and analysis we have presented here caution against equating this mobilization among abortion rights advocates with movement toward more majoritarian policy outcomes. The "folk theory of democracy" suggests that under these circumstances – where a clear majority of the public favors a specific policy outcome – the median voter is likely to prevail and improved representational outcomes will likely follow (Achen and Bartels 2017). Yet, due to the power and strategic influence of intense minorities and the hyperpolarization characterizing American politics at present, possibilities for policy change are significantly constrained.

The preferences and behavior of intense minorities are critical for understanding what comes next in American politics. Efforts to shift policy into congruence with public opinion will likely rely on an intense minority within the Democratic Party. This minority may be somewhat larger and more mobilized following the *Dobbs* decision, due to the heightened salience of conflict over abortion rights. Despite aligning more closely with majority opinion, this group will face many of the same obstacles the intense minority opposing abortion did when it gradually and persistently pursued changes that led to the present policy landscape (e.g., and unfavorable Supreme Court and status quo bias), along with some new ones (e.g., partisan gerrymandering and hyperpolarization). The path forward is likely to involve a sustained and incremental effort to rebuild rights at the state level.

In this section, we consider how preference intensity influenced voters' behavior in the first election following the *Dobbs* decision. Unfortunately, we do not have the same rich dataset of open-ended party evaluations to draw upon as in the previous sections, because such questions are only asked in presidential election years. However, we are able to evaluate media coverage of abortion to assess changes in issue salience, and we rely on past research on this topic to speculate about what these changes might mean for the role abortion plays in future elections. Additionally, we analyze data from the ANES pilot study to explore preference intensity in 2022 and its electoral implications. The results show the relationships between preference intensity and various forms of polarization we uncovered in the 2008 through 2020 elections persisted in 2022 and are likely to do so in future elections. To sum up our arguments, we revisit common mechanisms for policy influence and outline the obstacles facing future efforts to shape abortion policy.

Salience, Issue Importance, and Partisan Polarization in the 2022 Midterms

In earlier sections, we outlined how *Dobbs* altered the policy landscape, and in this section we turn to whether the decision impacted the role abortion plays in American elections. *Dobbs* undoubtedly heightened the salience of abortion rights among the American public just prior to the midterms. Past research shows that media coverage can have an agenda-setting effect (e.g., Dearing and

Rogers 1996), directing the public's attention to particular issues and making them more salient. A significant jump in the quantity of coverage surrounding an issue can also heighten public perceptions of an issue's importance and sharpen its influence on candidate evaluations and electoral behavior (Abramowitz 1995; Brody 1991). Campaigns can also shape the salience of issues and contribute to agenda setting because the news media tends to cover issues candidates stress in their campaigns (Hillygus and Shields 2008; West 2017). Beyond this, prior research points to an important relationship between salience and policy congruence, with heighted salience corresponding to improvements in policy-opinion congruence because candidates and elected officials pay more attention to voters' preferences on issues they identify as important (Lax and Phillips 2009; Page and Shapiro 2010). For these reasons, we take a brief look at how preference intensity influenced the 2022 elections before turning to the longer-term impact of *Dobbs* on electoral politics and policy congruence.

The *Dobbs* decision sparked a great deal of media coverage. The leaked draft in May of 2022 generated considerable attention as "the worst breach of confidentiality in the court's history" (e.g., de Vogue et al. 2023). The landmark quality of the official decision and its proximity to the midterms produced a spate of coverage as well. To get a sense of the changing salience of abortion in news media, we report monthly mentions of abortion in the *New York Times* between 2008 and 2022 in Figure 16.[57] Before 2022, the *Times* ran a monthly average of 47 stories mentioning abortion. This changed dramatically when the *Dobbs* decision leaked. In the first four months of 2022, the *New York Times* ran about 60 stories a month that mentioned abortion. By comparison, 293 stories mentioning abortion were published in May of 2022 alone, when the decision leaked initially, and the paper ran 319 stories in July, following the official judgment issued in late June. A comparable pattern of coverage was also evident in more right-leaning outlets, such as the *Wall Street Journal* (see Figure 17).[58]

Americans were also exposed to an increase in abortion messaging in campaign communications, particularly for office seekers from the Democrat Party. The *Washington Post* reported that abortion was the top issue mentioned among Democrats running for Congress in 2022. Based on data from AdImpact,

---

[57] We used a keyword search for abortion anywhere in the *New York Times* (Pubid 11561) and the *Wall Street Journal* (Pubid 10482) in the ProQuest Central database. Entries such as reviews, corrections, and obituaries were excluded. Each month's articles consist of briefs, commentary, opinions, editorials, and news.

[58] Overall, there are fewer articles mentioning abortion in the *Wall Street Journal* compared to the *New York Times*. Our analysis does not account for differences in the total number of stories on all topics reported in each paper, so we cannot determine whether changes in abortion coverage were proportional across outlets. Regardless, it is clear that media coverage of abortion intensified markedly due to the *Dobbs* decision for both outlets.

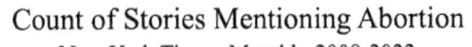

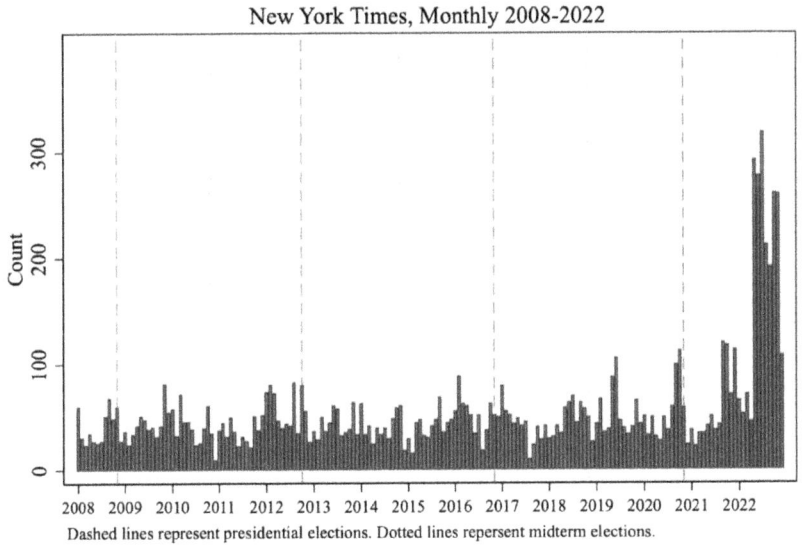

Abortion Attitudes and Polarization in the American Electorate 73

Figure 16 News coverage of abortion in the *New York Times*, 2008 to 2022

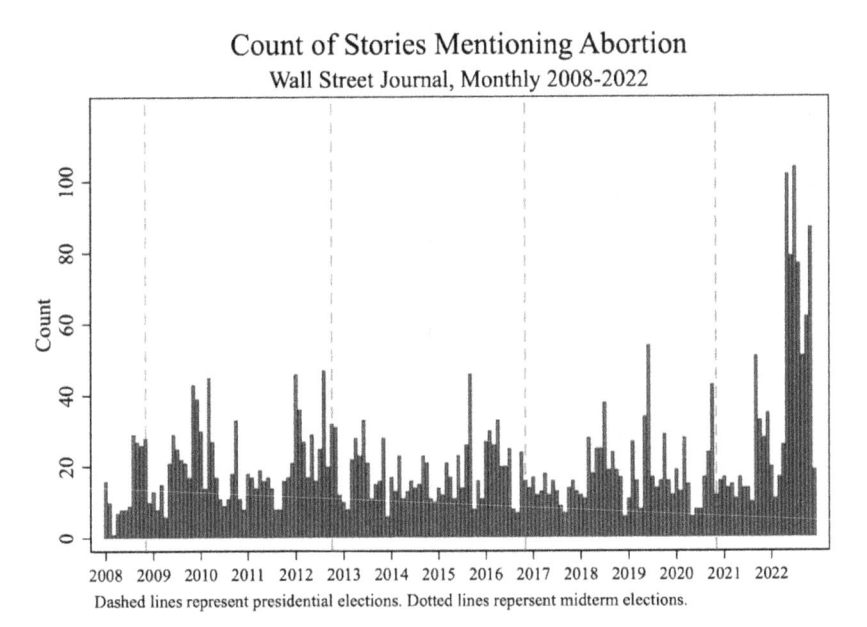

Figure 17 News coverage of abortion in the *Wall Street Journal*, 2008 to 2022

abortion was mentioned in 197,000 ad airings and represented $103,000,000 in spending for Democratic candidates. By comparison, Republican candidates aired only 11,000 ads referencing abortion, reflecting about $4,000,000 in spending (Stevens and Itkowitz 2022). Based on these figures, it is fair to say that abortion rights were salient in the information environment surrounding the 2022 midterms.

The bump in reporting and campaign communication involving abortion rights seemed to coincide with heightened issue importance as well, consistent with an agenda-setting effect. The 2022 ANES asked: "How important is [abortion] to you personally?" and then prompted responses on a 5-point Likert scale ranging from "not at all important" to "extremely important."[59] This question was also asked in 2020 and responses are reported alongside the 2022 data for comparison purposes in Figure 18. The figure shows small, but meaningful, differences pre- and post-*Dobbs*. In 2020, average personal importance ratings for Democrats and Republicans are roughly comparable; they differ by only 0.06 on the 5-point scale. In 2022, average personal importance scores

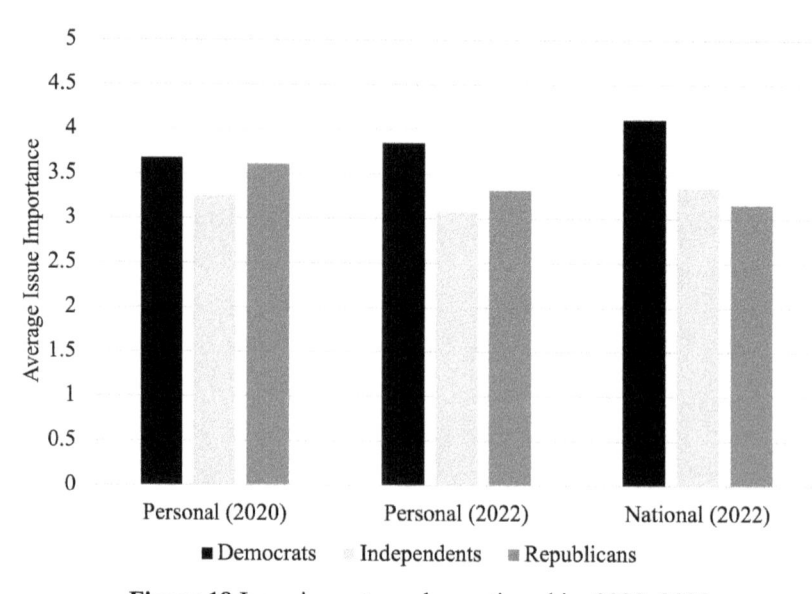

Figure 18 Issue importance by partisanship, 2020–2022

---

[59] The 2022 survey contained a randomized split-ballot experiment for this question in which a few of the labels on the response options varied slightly. Sensitivity analysis suggests this modest change did not appreciably alter our results.

increased for Democrats while decreasing among Republicans and the gap between the two groups grew to 0.48 – a statistically significant difference.[60]

The partisan gap is even more pronounced when looking at national importance – which unfortunately was asked only in 2022.[61] On this related measure, Democrats rate the issue nearly a full point higher than Republicans.[62] The same pattern was observed in exit polling as well. About 27 percent of voters nationwide indicated that abortion was the most important issue in determining their vote choice (CNN 2022). Of that group, 76 percent identified as Democrats. Republicans, by contrast, were more likely to cite crime, inflation, and immigration as the core issues shaping their vote decision. These differences point to an asymmetric reaction to *Dobbs*, with Democrats reacting more strongly to the decision as a major defeat for their side by rating the issue as more personally and nationally important compared to Republicans.

Though we have mentioned previously that "importance" may be an imperfect proxy for preference intensity, we are unable to use the same approach as in the previous section because party evaluations are only asked in presidential election years. Thus, to further investigate the relative intensity across party lines and the impact of intensity on electoral behavior, we rely on a proxy derived from these importance measures. We averaged responses to the two importance questions asked in 2022 (personal and national) and recoded the resulting measure into quartiles.[63] To demonstrate the impact of abortion focus in the analysis that follows, we compare survey respondents in the lowest quartile to those in the highest quartile.[64] We refer to these comparison groups as "high importance" and "low importance" rather than "abortion-focused" and "not abortion-focused" to remind the reader that we are using a proxy measure and to qualify direct comparisons with analysis from the previous section.

In 2022, about 58 percent of the high importance group identified with the Democratic Party, compared to 32 percent who identified as Republican. This difference is a departure from the partisan difference we observed in the pre-*Dobbs* period, where abortion-focused Republicans outnumbered abortion-focused Democrats nearly 2:1. In Section 6, we argued that intense minority influence was tied to the connection between preference intensity and polarization. Using our proxy measure, we observe the same types of relationships here, though in many cases they are more pronounced for Democrats relative to Republicans.

---

[60] The difference was evaluated using an Adjusted Wald test: $F(1,1497)=34.44$, $p<.001$.
[61] The distributions of responses to these items are provided in Table B1 of Appendix B.
[62] The difference was evaluated using an Adjusted Wald test: $F(1,1496)=108.91$, $p<.001$.
[63] The reliability for this two-item scale was alpha=.74.
[64] In essence, people in the upper quartile selected the "extremely important" option for both the personal and national salience item, whereas people in the lowest quartile indicated the issue was somewhat important, not too important, or not at all important on a personal and/or national level.

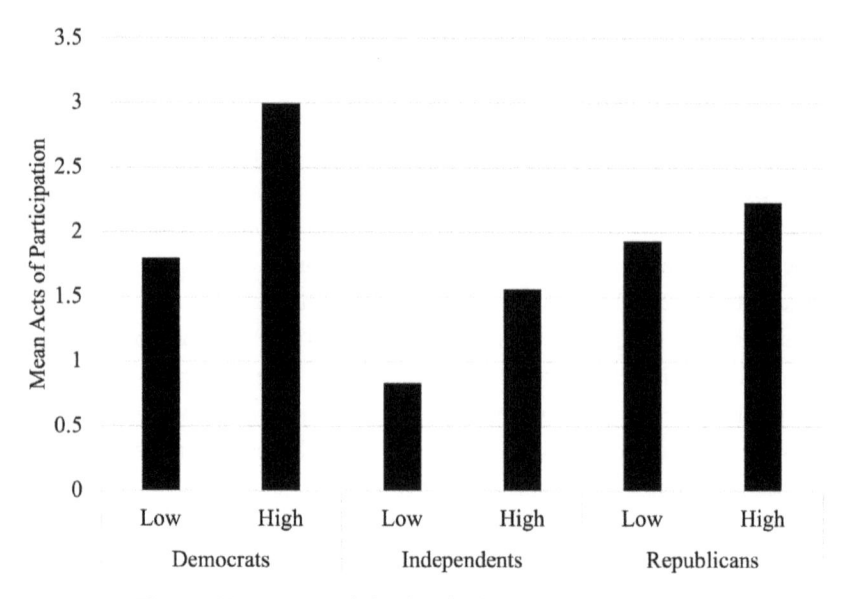

Figure 19 Mean participation by issue importance, 2022

First, in Figure 19, we see "high-importance" Democrats reported significantly greater levels of involvement in the campaign relative to those who placed little importance on the issue (2.99 acts of participation on average compared to 1.80), consistent with our prior findings on behavioral polarization.[65] Rates of voting were roughly comparable for these two groups of Democrats (83.9 percent and 77.3 percent); but those rating abortion as "high importance" were more likely to engage in the midterms in other capacities, such as attending meetings, displaying campaign materials, and donating to a candidate, party or related group. Republicans and independents, by contrast, participated in the midterms at comparable rates regardless of the importance of the issue. Looking briefly at gender differences within the parties, we found that of Republicans who felt abortion was of "high importance," 54.2 percent were female, and 45.8 percent were male. The gender difference was much more pronounced for Democrats. Of those scoring in the top quartile of the importance measure, 68.9 percent were female, and 31.2 percent were male. Thus, some of the asymmetry in mobilization across party lines is due to Democratic women with high preference intensity regarding abortion rights.[66]

---

[65] The difference in overall rates of participation for Democrats is significant: $F(1,736)=23.94$, $p<.001$. The difference in turnout is not: $\chi^2(2)=1.85$, $p=.28$.

[66] For more information about gender differences in public opinion on abortion see Barkan (2014), Lizotte (2015), Osborne et al. (2022) and both Table B2 and Figure B1 in Appendix B.

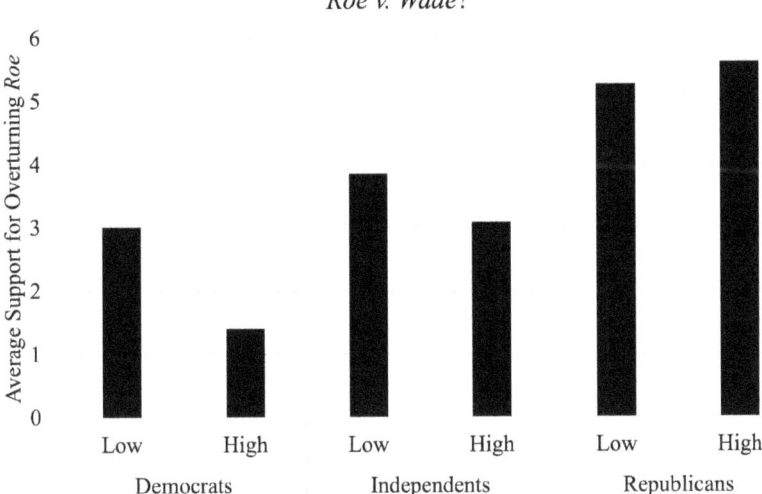

Abortion Attitudes and Polarization in the American Electorate

Do you favor or oppose the SCOTUS decision to overturn *Roe v. Wade*?

Figure 20 Positions on overturning *Roe*, 2022

The 2022 election survey included some items to gauge reactions to the recent *Dobbs* decision, and analysis of these questions provides further evidence of a connection between preference intensity, issue-based polarization, and affective polarization. For instance, survey participants were asked: "As you may know, the U.S. Supreme Court overturned *Roe v. Wade*, ruling that there is no constitutional right to abortion. Do you favor, oppose or neither favor nor oppose the Supreme Court's decision to overturn *Roe v. Wade*?" People who selected "favor" or "oppose" were asked a follow up question gauging intensity: a little, a moderate amount, a great deal. Responses to these questions were combined to form a 7-point Likert scale, and mean score by issue importance and party are depicted in Figure 20. For both Democrats and Republicans, partisans with high importance ratings hold more polarized preferences than those with low importance ratings, though the difference is only statistically significant for Democrats.[67]

This is not to say that issue importance is unrelated to abortion attitudes among Republicans, however. A look at the distribution of responses to the common abortion attitudes survey question we have evaluated in other sections shows a marked difference in preferences among Republicans based on preference intensity (see Table 7). Nearly 50 percent of Republicans who rate abortion

---

[67] The difference between high and low importance Democrats was statistically significant at the $p<.001$ level [$F(1,741)=31.52$].

Table 7 Partisanship, issue importance, and abortion attitudes, 2022

	Democrats		Independents		Republicans	
	Low	High	Low	High	Low	High
Never Permitted	9.75	4.22	10.21	19.95	3.87	49.77
Narrow Set of Cases	16.27	6.77	23.51	10.58	48.74	30.17
Broader Set of Cases	26.16	3.27	31.66	4.91	27.67	3.56
Always Permitted	47.83	85.75	34.63	64.56	19.72	16.49
	$\chi^2(3)=49.89, p<.001$		$\chi^2(3)=16.08, p<.01$		$\chi^2(3)=99.01, p<.001$	

Note: Entries are percentages. Survey weights are applied.

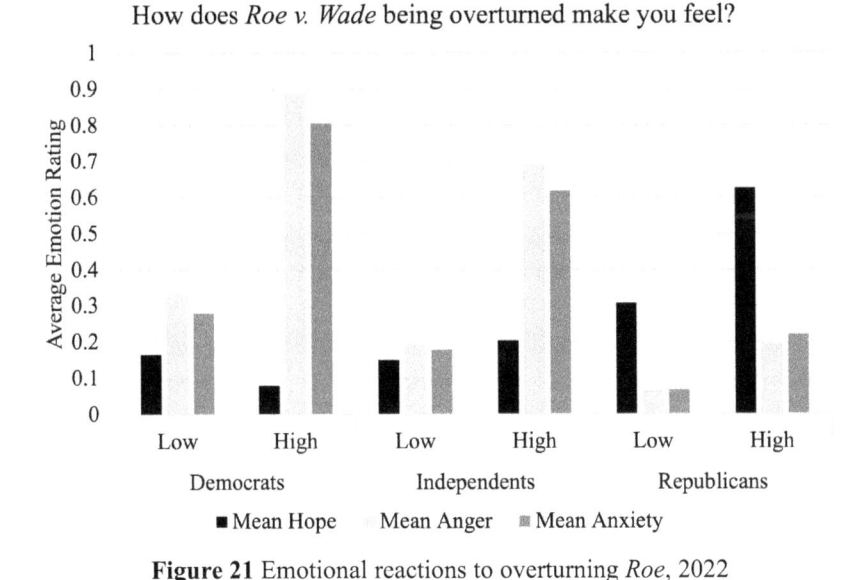

How does *Roe v. Wade* being overturned make you feel?

Figure 21 Emotional reactions to overturning *Roe*, 2022

as "high importance" feel it should never be permitted, compared to only 4 percent of Republicans who rate the issue as "low importance." These figures offer further support for the idea that people with intense preferences hold more extreme, or polarized, issue positions as well.

Survey respondents also provided information about their emotional reactions to the *Dobbs* decision (see Figure 21), and we can use this information to assess the relationship between preference intensity and affective polarization. As one might expect, hope was the dominant emotion among Republicans – yet hopeful responses were significantly more pronounced for Republicans who rated the issue as "high importance."[68] Anger and anxiety dominated the reactions of independents and Democrats and reached significantly higher levels among the "high importance" subsets of these groups.[69] This pattern of results points to very different levels of emotional investment at varying levels of issue importance, with voters who see abortion as a "high importance" issue reacting more strongly to the loss (for Democrats) or victory (for Republicans).

Collectively, our analysis of the 2022 ANES pilot points to continuity in the relationships between preference intensity and polarization in the pre- and post-*Dobbs* eras. Americans who place high importance on the issue participate more

---

[68] The difference was assessed using an Adjusted Wald Test [$F(1,741)=68.38$, $p<.001$].
[69] Significance test information for these contrasts is as follows: high/low importance independents – anger [$F(1,741)=36.51$, $p<.001$], high/low importance Democrats – anger [$F(1,741)=207.53$, $p<.001$], high/low importance independents – anxiety [$F(1,741)=30.87$, $p<.001$], and high/low importance Democrats – anxiety [$F(1,741)=179.03$, $p<.001$].

in politics, have stronger emotional reactions to policy change (an important precursor of political participation, e.g., Huddy et al. 2015; Valentino et al. 2011; Weber 2013), and hold somewhat more polarized preferences regarding policy as well. At the same time, we observed some evidence of asymmetric mobilization, with Democrats – and especially Democratic women – demonstrating uniquely high levels of engagement in the midterms.

Our brief look at the 2022 midterm elections demonstrates that *Dobbs* significantly changed the information environment regarding abortion through its impact on news media and the issues candidates stressed in their campaigns. We also showed that among voters who rated abortion as an important issue, both to them personally and to the nation as a whole, involvement in the campaign was quite high. These results suggest that rather than mobilizing a frustrated majority, as some journalists and pundits suggested, *Dobbs* may have activated and expanded an intense minority within the Democratic Party. The efforts of this group to shore up abortion rights may ultimately produce greater congruence between public opinion and policy, contributing to improved representational outcomes broadly over the long term. But an intense minority of abortion rights advocates will face some significant challenges in pursuing their policy goals. Next, we lay out these challenges, focusing on two potential pathways to improved policy congruence – elected representatives and direct ballot measures – and explore how efforts to secure abortion rights using these pathways will likely impact future elections.

Seeking Policy Congruence through Elected Representatives

Electoral accountability can be one path to policy change. Elections provide voters with an opportunity to replace representatives who are out of step with their preferences – particularly if these preferences are shared by a majority of voters within their district. As noted previously, the *Dobbs* decision increased coverage of abortion in the news media and bolstered the attention it received in congressional campaigns as well. Some might expect this to strengthen the potential for electoral accountability, and there is some evidence that abortion did loom large in the minds of voters when they showed up to the polls in 2022. In a survey conducted by the Kaiser Family Foundation just prior to the election, 38 percent of voters said abortion had a major impact on whether they decided to turn out to vote (and that figure was even higher among first-time voters, at 54 percent). Of this group, 47 percent said the issue had a major impact on the candidates they supported as well (KFF 2022).

But there are limitations to the ability of increased salience to widely activate the electorate in this way, and these limitations demonstrate how electoral accountability often falls short in practice. Voters generally lack the interest, knowledge, and civic competence needed to uphold their role in a representative democracy (Achen and Bartels 2017; Bishin 2009; Carpini and Keeter 1996). While abortion is more salient in 2022 than it was before *Dobbs*, it was still relatively salient prior (Bishin 2009; Lax and Phillips 2009), due to the events described in our policy history, and yet the public's knowledge about abortion has been relatively limited (Pagoto et al. 2023). And despite its heightened salience, abortion policy is complex and in flux. Journalists have noted that many Americans are unaware of how abortion bans, even when they have exceptions, limit healthcare options for pregnant persons (Romo 2023; Zernike 2024b). Beyond this, many Americans are uncertain as to the exact legal status of abortion in their home state (PRRI 2023). As a result, it is unclear whether the typical American is sufficiently informed or motivated to hold elected officials accountable on this issue, particularly if issue salience declines or if state-wide developments do not receive sufficient attention in the national media.

Overall rates of voter mobilization do not point to a significant shift due to *Dobbs*. Voter turnout was largely in line with the 2018 midterm elections – 46 percent of voters turned out in 2022 compared to 49 percent in 2018 (and about 66 percent in the 2020 presidential election, Hartig et al. 2023). In our analysis of the 2022 ANES pilot, we saw some evidence of mobilization related to abortion preferences, but it was largely confined to Democrats. This suggests that *Dobbs*, and the media coverage surrounding it, did not awaken a frustrated majority per se. Rather, it likely expanded an intense minority that is supportive of abortion rights. Media coverage of the midterms similarly emphasized mobilization in support of Democratic candidates and ballot measures related to abortion (e.g., KFF 2022). These accounts of asymmetric mobilization point to a shift in the relative electoral influence of intense minorities on either side of the debate over abortion rights. Pluralistic politics indicates that an expanding intense minority supporting abortion rights could offset the power of the intense minority that opposes them, potentially resulting in a compromise between these two sides that aligns with the majority viewpoint, though the current political environment complicates this dynamic. Ultimately, it is premature to say the issue has transformed the electorate in a meaningful and enduring fashion.

The role of candidates and their position-taking also warrants mention in terms of this pathway for influence. Office seekers are strategic actors; they can read the tea leaves and shift their platforms to try to widen their electoral appeal. However, the ability of candidates to respond is presently quite constrained. The high level of partisan polarization in today's political environment makes it harder for politicians to shift positions. Beyond this, some political scientists argue that partisanship has also become more rigid and calcified, which further limits the potential for candidates to moderate their positions (Sides et al. 2022). As discussed in Section 4, the Republican and Democratic parties have staked out distinct policy positions on abortions since the 1980s. The parties are further apart ideologically today than in previous decades, but they are also more homogeneous, and the hold of partisanship on both elites and voters has increased. While the threat of losing elections should motivate parties and politicians to moderate their positions, elites have established reputations and parties have mechanisms for policing their members, making it difficult to change positions on highly visible issues. Some office holders are also insulated from electoral pressures by institutional factors, such as partisan gerrymandering.

Yet the recent losses the Republican Party has faced when abortion is on the ballot may provide the impetus for them to try. As we enter the 2024 election cycle, there appears to be some movement among Republicans to moderate their positions on abortion (Bidgood and Lerer 2024). While former president Trump has continued to vocally claim credit for overturning *Roe*, in April of 2024, he announced on Truth Social that future abortion policy should be set by the states. If a federal ban were to come across his desk, he claimed he did not intend to sign it. This position seemed linked to Republican electoral losses. In another Truth Social post, the former president wrote: "Many Good Republicans lost Elections because of this Issue, and people like Lindsey Graham, that are unrelenting, are handing Democrats their dream of the House, Senate, and perhaps even the Presidency."

The former President's statements reflect a departure from the official position taken by the Republican Party, which has called for a constitutional amendment banning abortion in its party platforms since 1976. While it often seems like the former President is afforded more leeway than many politicians in shifting his issue positions, it is unclear whether he will successfully shift the positions of other Republicans. Many conservatives and anti-abortion activists have been highly critical of Trump's announcement (Ollstien 2024). Additionally, some elements of the party do not appear to be moderating their position on abortion at all, but rather are taking increasingly extreme positions. For instance, the Republican Party in the state of Texas recently adopted a platform stating, "Abortion is not healthcare, it is homicide" (Jamie 2024). While this platform does not explicitly state that abortion should be punishable by the death penalty, it does advocate for classifying an embryo or fetus as a preborn child. Because the murder of children under the age of fifteen is a capital offense in the state of Texas, abortion rights advocates are concerned about the downstream consequences of this change.

Other aspects of American political institutions will likely constrain the efforts of an intense minority of abortion rights advocates. Reliance on elected representation to secure policy change assumes electoral and legislative institutions operate according to democratic principles. Yet the integrity of these democratic institutions has eroded somewhat over time as a result of factors like partisan gerrymandering, voter suppression, and malapportionment (Levitsky and Ziblatt 2023). In many of the states where abortion policy poorly reflects the public's preferences, Republicans have used tools like redistricting to secure an advantage in the state legislature, which has facilitated an increase in countermajoritarian policy outcomes (Levitsky and Ziblatt 2023; Seifter 2021). The changes to these institutions will likely make it more difficult for abortion policy to become better aligned with public opinion.

The courts will continue to pose an obstacle to these efforts as well. As we discussed in Section 2, the Supreme Court often acts as the final arbitrator of abortion policies passed by the states, and the current docket suggests it will continue to shape abortion policy by ruling on issues related to the distribution of medication abortion and the relationship between state abortion bans and federal policy like the Emergency Medical Treatment and Labor Act (EMTALA), among other factors. The Supreme Court is isolated from electoral accountability and the forces that can sometimes pressure legislators to moderate their position. Not only do lifetime appointments eliminate electoral incentives, but they also make the composition of the Court stable and slow to change. And change will likely occur even more slowly than in the past, because justices are being appointed at a younger age and tend to live longer. For example, there were forty-seven appointments to the Court between 1917 and 2017, but it is estimated that there will only be twenty-five appointments between 2017 and 2117 (Fishbaum 2018). It took decades for the intense anti-abortion minority to overturn *Roe* by shifting the composition of the Court; however, it will likely take even longer for a pro-abortion minority to shift the composition of the Court significantly.

Seeking Policy Congruence through Direct Ballot Initiatives

Post-*Dobbs*, ballot initiatives have proven critical for protecting abortion rights in states where conservative legislatures sought to pass restrictive abortion laws not reflective of the public's preferences. Not only have these initiatives proven successful at improving policy congruence, but the boost in turnout in these elections suggests that placing abortion rights directly on the ballot can mobilize voters (Chinni 2022, KFF 2022). As a result, some have argued that similar initiatives should be part of the Democratic Party's strategy in 2024 (Mueller 2024). As of the writing of this Element, there are four states with confirmed ballot initiatives for the 2024 Presidential election (Colorado,

Florida, Maryland, and South Dakota) and nine states where the ballot initiative process was started but has yet to be finalized (Ballotpedia 2024b; Felix et al. 2024). While the specifics of the ballot measures vary state by state, these ballot initiatives may provide voters an opportunity to protect abortion rights.[70]

The use of ballot initiatives by supporters of abortion rights is something of a departure from past precedent. For decades, ballot initiatives have been a popular tool among those wishing to restrict policies at the state level. Before *Dobbs*, 80 percent of ballot initiatives were supported by anti-abortion organizations (Ballotpedia 2024c), and these measures were often effective at contributing to more conservative state policies (Caughey and Warshaw 2022). The focus of these initiatives has ranged from limiting the use of public funds for abortion to amending state constitutions pertaining to "fetal personhood." There is mixed evidence as to whether ballot initiatives generally promote policy congruence (Achen and Bartels 2017; Arceneaux 2002; Gerber 1996; Lax and Phillips 2012). Many scholars have found that these forms of direct democracy often do not produce majoritarian outcomes because they can be effectively leveraged by intense minorities and special interests to outmaneuver more diffuse and less attentive majorities (Achen and Bartels 2017; Ellis 2002; Haskell 2001).

But this path to influence is not available everywhere – there are only twenty-six states with some form of direct ballot or referendum option. And many of the states we identified as "misaligned" in terms of public opinion and policy in our Section 3 analysis lack the option for citizen initiated ballot measures (i.e., Alabama, Georgia, Indiana, Kentucky, Louisiana, North Carolina, South Carolina, Tennessee, and Texas).[71] Moreover, how these items are placed on the ballot and the number of votes needed for the measure to pass vary from state to state. In some states, citizens can place initiatives on the ballot directly, but others require the initiative to originate in the state legislature. This can raise the difficulty for securing majoritarian outcomes. For example, in 2024, voters in Florida will vote to protect abortion up to viability and, when necessary, to protect the life of a pregnant person. However, to add this protection to the Florida constitution, the initiative must receive the support of at least 60 percent of voters, more than just a mere majority. These examples highlight the challenges of pursuing policy congruence through ballot initiatives, even in an environment where the will of the majority is clear.

---

[70] Nebraska has four different measures in the process of being placed on the ballot: two would restrict abortion rights, and two would protect abortion rights (Ballotpedia 2024b).
[71] In Iowa, Pennsylvania, Wyoming, and Mississippi (states where opinion and policy were also misaligned) citizens cannot initiate direct ballot measures but the state legislature can.

Conclusion

The Supreme Court's decision in *Dobbs* and subsequent actions to further restrict abortion rights taken by many states are troubling because they fail to reflect majority opinion, which is largely supportive of abortion in at least some circumstances. In this Element, we sought to better understand how the United States arrived at the current level of misalignment between abortion policy and public opinion. We relied on Hill's (2022) prior scholarship on frustrated majorities to explicate the role of preference intensity in this process. Centering the attitudes of abortion-focused Americans in our analysis not only provided insights into the circumstances contributing to the *Dobbs* decision, it also offered a deeper understanding of the connection between abortion and broader patterns of polarization in the American electorate.

Ultimately, the policy landscape post-*Dobbs* is not dissimilar from the landscape prior to *Roe v. Wade*. *Dobbs* triggered a reversion to the states as a locus of policymaking, and the resulting patchwork of laws has created an atmosphere of ambiguity regarding what is legal and who can access abortion care across the states (McCann 2023; KFF 2023). The key difference between the pre-*Roe* and post-*Dobbs* periods is the heightened level of partisan polarization. The Supreme Court's decision in *Roe* set in motion a partisan realignment that bound abortion attitudes and partisanship more closely together. Both polarization and preference intensity are critical for understanding the impact the *Dobbs* decision will have on electoral politics moving forward.

Our look at the 2022 midterms with an eye toward the 2024 presidential election suggests things may be shifting. In past election years, abortion-focused Republicans outnumbered abortion-focused Democrats, but data from the 2022 ANES pilot study suggest a recent reversal. And this finding tracks with other survey data collected around the same time. For instance, the Kaiser Family Foundation reported that 37 percent of Democrats said abortion was the single most important factor in their vote, compared to only 13 percent of Republicans (KFF 2022).

Collectively, this points to the expansion of an intense minority in support of abortion rights. However, it took decades for the opponents of abortion rights to achieve success. Given the slow nature of political change in the United States, the current composition of the Supreme Court, and the challenges associated with securing change through elected officials and direct ballot measures outlined here, progress is likely to be slow and incremental. Sustained mobilization will be necessary to shift abortion policy back in abortion-focused Democrats' preferred direction.

The power of intense minorities to shape institutions and policy illustrated in this Element highlights the importance of citizen engagement. Diffuse majorities are often easily sidelined by intense minorities willing to engage in costly political behavior. As a result, it is important for citizens invested in an issue like abortion to focus on the types of behavior that send a clear signal to political elites and offer the best chance of influencing policy (Hersh 2020). And, it is crucial to understand how the broader political context factors in as well. Many of the obstacles currently facing proponents of abortion rights are tied up in larger problems related to democratic backsliding and the erosion of democratic norms. Efforts to shore up American democracy are likely to bolster abortion rights as well.

References

Abortion – In Depth Topics. 2024. Gallup (January 3). https://news.gallup.com/poll/1576/abortion.aspx.

Abramowitz, Alan I. 1995. "It's Abortion, Stupid: Policy Voting in the 1992 Presidential Election." *The Journal of Politics* 57(1): 176–186.

Abramowitz, Alan I. 2010. *The Disappearing Center: Engaged Citizens, Polarization, and American Democracy*. New Haven, CT: Yale University Press.

Achen, Christopher, and Larry Bartels. 2017. *Democracy for Realists: Why Elections Do Not Produce Responsive Government*. Princeton, NJ: Princeton University Press.

Adams, Greg D. 1997. "Abortion: Evidence of an Issue Evolution." *American Journal of Political Science* 41(3): 718–737.

Adkins, Savannah, Noa Tolmor, Molly H. White, Cryan Dutton, and Ashely L. O'Donoghue. 2024. "Association between Restricted Abortion Access and Child Entries into the Foster Care System." *JAMA Pediatrics* 178(1): 37–44.

Akron v. Akron Center for Reproductive Health, 462 U.S. 416. 1983. https://supreme.justia.com/cases/federal/us/462/416.

Allen, Jonathan, Marc Caputo, and Scott Wong. 2022. "'Bad Idea': Republicans Pan Lindsey Graham's 15-Week Abortion Ban." *NBC News* (September 13). www.nbcnews.com/politics/congress/sen-graham-introduces-bill-ban-abortion-nationwide-15-weeks-rcna47530.

American Historical Association. 2022. "History, the Supreme Court, and *Dobbs v. Jackson*: Joint Statement from the American Historical Association and the Organization of American Historians." (July 6). https://www.historians.org/news/history-the-supreme-court-and-dobbs-v-jackson-joint-statement-from-the-aha-and-the-oah/.

Arceneaux, Kevin. 2002 "Direct Democracy and the Link between Public Opinion and State Abortion Policy." *State Politics & Policy Quarterly* 2(4): 372–387.

Arnold, Grace. 2022. "The Impact of Targeted Regulation of Abortion Providers Laws on Abortions and Girths." *Journal of Population Economics* 35(4): 1443–1472.

Ballotpedia. 2024a. "States with Initiative or Referendum." (May 15). https://ballotpedia.org/States_with_initiative_or_referendum.

Ballotpedia. 2024b. "2024 Abortion-Related Ballot Measures and State Context." (June 9). https://ballotpedia.org/2024_abortion-related_ballot_measures_and_state_context.

Ballotpedia. 2024c. "History of Abortion Ballot Measures." (June 9). https://ballotpedia.org/History_of_abortion_ballot_measures.

Balmer, Randall. 2021. *Bad Faith: Race and the Rise of the Religious Right*. Grand Rapids, MI: Wm. B. Eerdmans.

Banaszak, Lee Ann, and Heather L. Ondercin. 2016. "Explaining the Dynamics between the Women's Movement and the Conservative Movement in the United States." *Social Forces* 95(1): 381–410.

Barkan, Steven E. 2014. "Gender and Abortion Attitudes: Religiosity as a Suppressor Variable." *Public Opinion Quarterly* 78(4): 940–950.

Bartels, Brandon L., and Christopher D. Johnston. 2013. "On the Ideological Foundations of Supreme Court Legitimacy in the American Public." *American Journal of Political Science* 57(1): 184–199.

Bawn, Kathleen, Martin Cohen, David Karol et al. 2012. "A Theory of Political Parties: Groups, Policy Demands and Nominations in American Politics." *Perspectives on Politics* 10(3): 571–597.

Belluck, Pam. 2024. "Five Takeaways from the Supreme Court Arguments on Idaho's Abortion Ban." *The New York Times* (April 24). www.nytimes.com/2024/04/24/us/politics/supreme-court-idaho-abortion-law.html.

Bentele, Keith Gunnar, Rebecca Sager, and Amanda Aykanian. 2018. "Rewinding *Roe v. Wade*: Understanding the Accelerated Adoption of State-level Restrictive Abortion Legislation, 2008–2014." *Journal of Women, Politics & Policy* 39(4): 490–517.

Bidgood, Jess, and Lisa Lerer. 2024. "How Republicans in Key Senate Races Are Flip-Flopping on Abortion." *The New York Times* (May 30). www.nytimes.com/2024/05/30/us/politics/republican-senate-races-abortion.html.

Bishin, Benjamin. 2009. *Tyranny of the Minority: The Subconstituency Politics Theory of Representation*. Philadelphia, PA: Temple University Press.

Black, Ryan C., Ryan J. Owens, Justin Wedeking, and Patrick C. Wohlfarth. 2016. "The Influence of Public Sentiment on Supreme Court Opinion Clarity." *Law & Society Review* 50(3): 703–732.

Blake, Judith. 1971. "Abortion and Public Opinion: The 1960–1970 Decade." *Science* 171(3971): 540–549.

Bonilla, Tabitha. 2022. *The Importance of Campaign Promises*. Cambridge: Cambridge University Press.

Brady, David, Bruce Cain, Kim Fridkin et al. 2023. Abortion – A joint polling project among researchers at Arizona State University, Stanford University, and the University of Houston. https://uh.edu/hobby/jointpollingproject_abortion.

References

Brenan, Megan. 2018. "Gallup Vault: Public Supported Therapeutic Abortion in 1962." Gallup (June 12). https://news.gallup.com/vault/235496/gallup-vault-public-supported-therapeutic-abortion-1962.aspx.

Brody, Richard. 1991. *Assessing the President: The Media, Elite Opinion, and Public Support*. Stanford, CA: Stanford University Press.

Camobreco, John F., and Michelle A. Barnello. 2008. "Democratic Responsiveness and Policy Shock: The Case of State Abortion Policy." *State Politics & Policy Quarterly* 8(1): 48–65.

Campbell, David E., and Christina Wolbrecht. 2006. "See Jane Run: Women Politicians as Role Models for Adolescents." *The Journal of Politics* 68(2): 233–247.

Carmines, Edward G., and James A. Stimson. 1989. *Issue Evolution: Race and the Transformation of American Politics*. Princeton, NJ: Princeton University Press.

Carmines, Edward G., and James Woods. 2002. "The Role of Party Activists in the Evolution of the Abortion Issue." *Political Behavior* 24(4): 361–377.

Carmines, Edward G., Jessica C. Gerrity, and Michael W. Wagner. 2010. "How Abortion Became a Partisan Issue: Media Coverage of the Interest Group-Political Party Connection." *Politics & Policy* 38(6): 1135–1158.

Carpini, Michael X. Delli, and Scott Keeter. 1996. *What Americans Know about Politics and Why It Matters*. New Haven, CT: Yale University Press.

Caughey, Devin, and Christopher Warshaw. 2022. *Dynamic Democracy: Public Opinion, Elections, and Policymaking in the American States*. Chicago, IL: University of Chicago Press.

Center for Reproductive Rights. 2023a. "Legal Analysis What *Dobbs* Got Wrong." (March 15). https://reproductiverights.org/wp-content/uploads/2023/03/Legal-Analysis-What-Dobbs-Got-Wrong-3.15.23.pdf.

Center for Reproductive Rights. 2023b. "Texas Abortion Ban Emergency Exceptions Case: *Zurawski v. The State of Texas*." (March 6). https://reproductiverights.org/case/zurawski-v-texas-abortion-emergency-exceptions/zurawski-v-texas.

Center for Reproductive Rights. 2024. "After *Roe* Fell: Abortion Laws by State." (January 3). https://reproductiverights.org/maps/abortion-laws-by-state.

Chinni, Dante. 2022. "Kansas Abortion Vote Offers Clues for the Midterms." *NBC News* (August 7). www.nbcnews.com/meet-the-press/kansas-abortion-vote-offers-clues-midterms-n1297759.

CNN. 2022. "2022 Exit Polls." www.cnn.com/election/2022/exit-polls/national-results/general/us-house/0.

Cohen, Marty, David Karol, Hans Noel, and John Zaller. 2009. *The Party Decides Presidential Nominations before and after Reform*. Chicago, IL: University of Chicago Press.

de Vogue, Ariane, Tierney Sneed, and Devan Cole. 2023. "Supreme Court Issues Report on *Dobbs* Leak but Says It Hasn't Identified the Leaker." *CNN* (January 19). www.cnn.com/2023/01/19/politics/supreme-court-dobbs-report-leak/index.html#.

Dearing, James W., and Everett M. Rogers. 1996. *Agenda-Setting*. Vol. 6. Thousand Oaks, CA: Sage.

Deckman, Melissa, Laurel Elder, Steven Greene, and Mary-Kate Lizotte. 2024. "Deceptively Stable? How the Stability of Aggregate Abortion Attitudes Conceals Partisan Induced Shifts." *Political Research Quarterly* 77(2): 500–517.

Democratic Party Platform. 1976. The American Presidency Project. www.presidency.ucsb.edu/documents/1976-democratic-party-platform.

Democratic Party Platform. 1980. The American Presidency Project. www.presidency.ucsb.edu/documents/1980-democratic-party-platform.

Dobbs v. Jackson Women's Health Organization, No. 19–1392, 597 US 215. 2022. https://supreme.justia.com/cases/federal/us/597/19-1392/.

Downs, Anthony. 1957. *An Economic Theory of Democracy*. New York: Harper and Row.

Dyck, Joshua J., and Shanna Pearson-Merkowitz. 2023. *The Power of Partisanship*. New York: Oxford University Press.

Eisenstadt v. Baird, 405 US, 438. 1972. https://supreme.justia.com/cases/federal/us/405/438.

Ellis, Richard J. 2002. *Democratic Delusions*. Lawrence, KS: University Press of Kansas.

Elving, Ron. 2018. "What Happened with Merrick Garland in 2016 and Why It Matters." *NPR* (June 29). www.npr.org/2018/06/29/624467256/what-happened-with-merrick-garland-in-2016-and-why-it-matters-now.

Enders, Adam M., and Robert N. Lupton. 2021. "Value Extremity Contributes to Affective Polarization in the US." *Political Science Research and Methods* 9(4): 857–866.

Erikson, Robert S., Gerald C. Wright, and John P. McIver. 1993. *Statehouse Democracy: Public Opinion and Policy in the American States*. Cambridge: Cambridge University Press.

FDA Questions and Answers on Mifepristone for Termination of Pregnancy Through Ten Weeks Gestation. 2023. Food and Drug Administration

(September 1). www.fda.gov/drugs/postmarket-drug-safety-information-patients-and-providers/questions-and-answers-mifepristone-medical-termination-pregnancy-through-ten-weeks-gestation#LitigationandOtherLegalIssue.

Feddersen, Timothy J., Itai Sened, and Stephen G. Wright. 1990. "Rational Voting and Candidate Entry under Plurality Rule." *American Journal of Political Science* 34(4): 1005–1016.

Felix, Mabel, Laurie Sobel, and Alina Salganicoff. 2024. "Addressing Abortion Access through State Ballot Initiatives." KFF (February 9). www.kff.org/womens-health-policy/issue-brief/addressing-abortion-access-through-state-ballot-initiatives/.

Fishbaum, David. 2018. "The Supreme Court Has a Longevity Problem, but Term Limits on Justices Won't Solve It." *Harvard Business Review* (July 13). https://hbr.org/2018/07/the-supreme-court-has-a-longevity-problem-but-term-limits-on-justices-wont-solve-it.

Flemming, Roy B., and B. Dan Wood. 1997. "The Public and the Supreme Court: Individual Justice Responsiveness to American Policy Moods." *American Journal of Political Science* 41(2): 468–498.

Foster, Diana Greene, M. Antonia Biggs, Lauren Ralph et al. 2022. "Socioeconomic Outcomes of Women Who Receive and Women Who Are Denied Wanted Abortions in the United States." *American Journal of Public Health* 112(9): 1290–1296.

Freeman, Jo. 1987. "Whom You Know versus Whom You Represent: Feminist Influence in the Democratic and Republican Parties." In M. F. Katzenstein and C. Mueller (Eds.), *The Women's Movements of the United States and Western Europe: Consciousness, Political Opportunity, and Public Policy*. Philadelphia, PA: Temple University Press, pp. 215–244.

Gerber, Elisabeth R. 1996. "Legislative Response to the Threat of Popular Initiatives." *American Journal of Political Science* 40(1): 99–128.

Giles, Micheal W., Bethany Blackstone, and Richard L. Vinning. 2008. "The Supreme Court in American Democracy: Unraveling the Linkages between Public Opinion and Judicial Decision Making." *The Journal of Politics* 70(2): 293–306.

Goodman, J. David. 2023a. "Texas Supreme Court Rules against Woman Who Sought Court-Approved Abortion." *The New York Times* (December 11). www.nytimes.com/2023/12/11/us/texas-abortion-kate-cox.html.

Goodman, J. David. 2023b. "Abortion Ruling Keeps Texas Doctors Afraid of Persecution." *The New York Times* (December 13). www.nytimes.com/2023/12/13/us/texas-abortion-doctor-prosecution.html.

GovTrack.us. 1976. "On a Separate Vote in the House, to Agree to the Hyde Amendment to H.R. 14232, which Prohibits the Use of Funds in the Bill to

Pay for or to Promote Abortions." GovTrack (June 24). www.govtrack.us/ congress/votes/94-1976/h952.

GovTrack.us. 1983. "To Pass S.J. Res. 3, Am Measure Amending the Constitution to Establish Legislative Authority in Congress and the States with Respect to Abortion, thereby Overturning the Supreme Court's Decision in Roe vs. Wade. Motion Failed; ⅔ Required." GovTrack (June 28). www .govtrack.us/congress/votes/98-1983/s169.

Gramlich, John. 2021. "How Trump Compared with Other Recent Presidents in Appointing Federal Judges." Pew Research Center (January 13). www.pewre search.org/short-reads/2021/01/13/how-trump-compares-with-other-recent-presidents-in-appointing-federal-judges.

Green, Emma. 2022. "How the Federalist Society Won." *The New Yorker* (July 24). www.newyorker.com/news/annals-of-education/how-the-federal ist-society-won.

Griswold v. Connecticut, 381 U.S. 479. 1965. https://supreme.justia.com/cases/ federal/us/381/479/.

Grossmann, Matt, and David A. Hopkins. 2016. *Asymmetric Politics: Ideological Republicans and Group Interest Democrats*. New York: Oxford University Press.

Grumbach, Jake. 2022. "The Supreme Court Just Rolled Democracy Back. You Can Measure How Much." *Politico* (June 30). www.politico.com/news/maga zine/2022/06/30/court-made-america-less-democratic-00043549.

Guttmacher Institute. 2023. "Abortion Bans in Cases of Sex or Race Selection or Genetic Anomaly." State Laws and Policies (August 31). www.guttma cher.org/state-policy/explore/abortion-bans-cases-sex-or-race-selection-or-genetic-anomaly.

Hall, Matthew E. K. 2014. "The Semiconstrained Court: Public Opinion, the Separation of Powers, and the US Supreme Court's Fear of Non-Implementation." *American Journal of Political Science* 58(2): 352–366.

Hansen, Susan B. 1997. "Talking about Politics: Gender and Contextual Effects on Political Proselytizing." *The Journal of Politics* 59(1): 73–103.

Harris v. McRae, 448 U.S. 297. 1980. https://supreme.justia.com/cases/federal/ us/448/297/.

Harrison, Steve. 2023. "Republicans Have North Carolina House Supermajority after Rep. Tricia Cotham Switch." *NPR* (April 5). www.npr.org/2023/04/05/ 1168256827/republicans-have-north-carolina-house-supermajority-after-rep-tricia-cotham-swit#:.

Hartig, Hannah, Andrew Daniller, Scott Keeter, and Ted Van Green. 2023. "Republican Gains in 2022 Midterms Driven Mostly by Turnout Advantage."

References

Pew Research Center (July 23). www.pewresearch.org/politics/2023/07/12/republican-gains-in-2022-midterms-driven-mostly-by-turnout-advantage.

Haskell, John. 2001. *Direct Democracy or Representative Government?* Boulder, CO: Westview

Haugeberg, Karissa. 2017. *Women against Abortion: Inside the Largest Moral Reform Movement of the Twentieth Century.* Champaign, IL: University of Illinois Press.

Henson, Jim, and Joshua Blank. 2022. New UT/Texas Politics Project Poll Press Release. (August 10). University of Texas – Texas Politics Project. www.texastribune.org/2022/08/10/texas-politics-project-abortion-polling.

Hersh, Eitan. 2020. *Politics Is for Power: How to Move beyond Political Hobbyism, Take Action, and Make Real Change.* New York, NY: Scribner

Hesketh, Therese, Li Lu, and Zhu Wei Xing. 2011. "The Consequences of Son Preference and Sex-Selective Abortion in China and Other Asian Countries." *Canadian Medical Association Journal* 183(12): 1374–1377.

Hill, Seth J. 2022. *Frustrated Majorities: How Issue Intensity Enables Smaller Groups of Voters to Get What They Want.* Cambridge: Cambridge University Press.

Hillygus, D. Sunshine, and Todd G. Shields. 2008. *The Persuadable Voter: Wedge Issues in Presidential Campaigns.* Princeton, NJ: Princeton University Press.

Hout, Michael, Stuart Perrett, and Sarah K. Cowan. 2022. "Stasis and Sorting of Americans' Abortion Opinions: Political Polarization Added to Religious and Other Differences." *Socius* 8: 1–11. https://doi.org/10.1177/23780231221117648.

Huddy, Leonie, Lilliana Mason, and Lene Aarøe. 2015. "Expressive Partisanship: Campaign Involvement, Political Emotion, and Partisan Identity." *American Political Science Review* 109(1): 1–17.

Iyengar, Shanto, and Masha Krupenkin. 2018. "The Strengthening of Partisan Affect." *Political Psychology* 39(1): 201–218.

Iyengar, Shanto, and Sean J. Westwood. 2015. "Fear and Loathing across Party Lines: New Evidence on Group Polarization." *American Journal of Political Science* 59(3): 690–707.

Iyengar, Shanto, Gaurav Sood, and Yphtach Lelkes. 2012. "Affect, Not Ideology: A Social Identity Perspective on Polarization." *Public Opinion Quarterly* 76(3): 405–431.

Jamie, Angie. 2024. "Potential Texas GOP Platform Suggests Death Penalty for Abortion Patients." *Teen Vogue* (May 31). www.teenvogue.com/story/potential-texas-gop-platform-suggests-death-penalty-for-abortion-patients.

Jessee, Stephen, Neil Malhotra, and Maya Sen. 2022. "A Decade-Long Longitudinal Survey Shows That the Supreme Court Is Now Much More Conservative Than the Public." *PNAS* 119(24): 1–7.

Johnson, Ben, and Logan Strother. 2021. "Trends: The Supreme Court's (Surprising?) Indifference to Public Opinion." *Political Research Quarterly* 74(1): 18–34.

Jones, Rachel K., and Jenna Jerman. 2014. "Abortion Incidence and Service Availability in the United States, 2014." *Perspectives on Sexual and Reproductive Health* 49(1): 17–27.

Kastellec, Jonathan P. 2018. "How Courts Structure State-Level Representation." *State Politics & Policy Quarterly* 18(1): 27–60.

KFF. 2022. "Analysis Reveals How Abortion Boosted Democratic Candidates in Tuesday's Midterm Election." Kaiser Family Foundation Report (November 11). www.kff.org/other/press-release/analysis-reveals-how-abortion-boosted-democratic-candidates-in-tuesdays-midterm-election/.

KFF. 2023. "The Public, Including Women of Childbearing Age, Are Largely Confused about the Legality of Medication Abortion and Emergency Contraceptives in Their States." Kaiser Family Foundation News Release (February 1). www.kff.org/womens-health-policy/press-release/the-public-including-women-of-childbearing-age-are-largely-confused-about-the-legality-of-medication-abortion-and-emergency-contraceptives-in-their-states/.

Killian, Mitchell, and Clyde Wilcox. 2008. "Do Abortion Attitudes Lead to Party Switching?" *Political Research Quarterly* 61(4): 561–573.

Klar, Samar, and Yanna Krupnikov. 2016. *Independent Politics*. Cambridge: Cambridge University Press.

Kreitzer, Rebecca J. 2015. "Politics and Morality in State Abortion Policy." *State Politics & Policy Quarterly* 15(1): 41–66.

LaRoche, Kathryn J., Kristen N. Jozkowski, Brandon L. Crawford, and Frederica Jackson. 2024. "Can Someone Be Both Pro-life and Pro-choice? Results from a National Survey of US Adults." *Perspectives on Sexual and Reproductive Health*. [Firstview]: 1–10.

Lax, Jeffrey R., and Justin H. Phillips. 2009. "How Should We Estimate Public Opinion in the States?" *American Journal of Political Science* 53(1): 107–121.

Lax, Jeffrey R., and Justin H. Phillips. 2012. "The Democratic Deficit in the States." *American Journal of Political Science* 56(1): 148–166.

Layman, Geoffrey C., and Thomas M. Carsey. 1998. "Why Do Party Activists Convert? An Analysis of Individual-Level Change on the Abortion Issue." *Political Research Quarterly* 51(3): 723–749.

Levendusky, Matthew. 2009. *The Partisan Sort: How Liberals Became Democrats and Conservatives Became Republicans*. Chicago, IL: University of Chicago Press.

Levitsky, Steven, and Daniel Ziblatt. 2023. *Tyranny of the Minority: Why American Democracy Reached the Breaking Point*. New York: Crown.

Lewis, Anthony. 1959. "Legal Abortions Proposed in Code; Law Institute Draft Restricts Use and Curbs Imposition of the Death Penalty." *The New York Times* (May 22). www.nytimes.com/1959/05/22/archives/legal-abortions-proposed-in-code-law-institute-draft-restricts-use.html?searchResultPosition=6.

Lizotte, Mary Kate. 2015. "The Abortion Attitudes Paradox: Model Specification and Gender Differences." *Journal of Women, Politics & Policy* 36(1): 22–42.

Luker, Kristin. 1984. *Abortion and the Politics of Motherhood*. Berkeley, CA: University of California Press.

Luthra, Shefali. 2024. "What Is the Comstock Act?" *The 19th* (March 25). https://19thnews.org/2024/03/what-is-the-comstock-act/.

Lysen, Dylan, Laura Ziegler, and Blaise Mesa. 2022. "Kansas Voters Decide to Keep Abortion Legal in the State, Rejecting an Amendment." *NPR* (August 3). www.npr.org/sections/2022-live-primary-election-race-results/2022/08/02/1115317596/kansas-voters-abortion-legal-reject-constitutional-amendment.

Maher v. Roe, 432 US 464. 1977. https://supreme.justia.com/cases/federal/us/432/464/.

Martel, Francois Alexi, Michael Buhrmester, Angel Gómez, Alexandra Vázquez, and William B. Swann Jr. 2021. "Why True Believers Make the Ultimate Sacrifice: Sacred Values, Moral Convictions, or Identity Fusion?" *Frontiers in Psychology* 15(12): 1–12.

Mason, Lilliana. 2018. *Uncivil Agreement: How Politics Became Our Identity*. Chicago, IL: University of Chicago Press.

McCann, Allison. 2022. "'Chaos and Confusion' in States Where Abortion Is On Again, Off Again." *The New York Times* (August 11). www.nytimes.com/interactive/2022/08/11/us/abortion-states-legal-illegal.html.

Mernyk, Joseph S., Sophia L. Pink, James N. Druckman, and Robb Willer. 2022. "Correcting Inaccurate Metaperceptions Reduces Americans' Support for Partisan Violence." *Proceedings of the National Academy of Sciences* 119(16): 1–9.

Miller, Sarah, Laura R. Wherry, and Diana Greene Foster. 2023. "The Economic Consequences of Being Denied an Abortion." *American Economic Journal: Economic Policy* 15(1): 394–437.

Minnesota Department of Health. 2023. *Reproductive Rights and Protections in Minnesota* (November 7). www.health.state.mn.us/people/womeninfants/abortion/index.html.

Mohr, James C. 1978. *Abortion in America: The Origins and Evolution of National Policy.* New York: Oxford University Press.

Mueller, Julia. 2024. "Democrats Seek Boost from Abortion Ballot Measures in Key Battlegrounds." *The Hill* (March 30). https://thehill.com/homenews/campaign/4564341-democrats-abortion-ballot-measure-arizona-new-york-montana-jon-tester-kari-lake-larry-hogan/.

Nash, Elizabeth, and Isabel Guarnieri. 2022. "13 States Have Abortion Trigger Bans – Here's What Happens When *Roe* Is Overturned." Guttmacher Institute (June 6). Policy Brief. www.guttmacher.org/article/2022/06/13-states-have-abortion-trigger-bans-heres-what-happens-when-roe-overturned.

National Abortion Federation. 2024. "Provider Security." https://prochoice.org/our-work/provider-security.

Noel, Hans. 2014. *Political Ideologies and Political Parties in America.* Cambridge: Cambridge University Press.

Norrander, Barbara. 2001. "Measuring State Public Opinion with the Senate National Election Study." *State Politics & Policy Quarterly* 1(1): 111–125.

Norrander, Barbara, and Clyde Wilcox. 1999. "Public Opinion and Policymaking in the States: The Case of Post-*Roe* Abortion Policy." *Policy Studies Journal* 27(4): 707–722.

Norrander, Barbara, and Clyde Wilcox. 2023. "Trends in Abortion Attitudes: From *Roe* to *Dobbs*." *Public Opinion Quarterly* 87(2): 427–458.

Ollstien, Alice Miranda. 2024. "Conservatives Clash with Trump on Leaving Abortion up to Voters." *Politico* (April 12). www.politico.com/news/2024/04/12/conservatives-trump-abortion-voters-states-00151866.

Ondercin, Heather Louise, and Mary Kate Lizotte. 2021. "You've Lost That Loving Feeling: How Gender Shapes Affective Polarization." *American Politics Research* 49(3): 282–292.

Osborne, Danny, Yanshu Huang, Nickola C. Overall et al. 2022. "Abortion Attitudes: An Overview of Demographic and Ideological Differences." *Political Psychology* 43: 29–76.

Page, Benjamin I., and Robert Y. Shapiro. 2010. *The Rational Public: Fifty Years of Trends in Americans' Policy Preferences.* Chicago, IL: University of Chicago Press.

Pagoto, Sherry L., Lindsay Palmer, and Nate Horwitz-Willis. 2023. "The Next Infodemic: Abortion Misinformation." *Journal of Medical Internet Research* 25: 1–6.

Paris, Francesca, and Nate Cohn. 2022. "After *Roe*'s End, Women Surged in Signing Up to Vote in Some States." *The New York Times* (August 25). www.nytimes.com/interactive/2022/08/25/upshot/female-voters-dobbs.html.

References

PerryUndam. 2022. "On the Cusp of Change: What to Know about Abortion in 2022." Key Findings from the National Survey of Voters Conducted by Perry Undam (February 23). https://perryundem.com/wp-content/uploads/2022/02/PerryUndem-Abortion-Public-Opinion-Survey-2022.pdf.

Pew Research Center. 2022. "Abortion Rises in Importance as a Voting Issue, Driven by Democrats." (August 23). www.pewresearch.org/politics/2022/08/23/abortion-rises-in-importance-as-a-voting-issue-driven-by-democrats/.

Pew Research Center. 2024. "Changing Partisan Coalitions in a Politically Divided Nation." (April 9). www.pewresearch.org/politics/2024/04/09/changing-partisan-coalitions-in-a-politically-divided-nation/.

Planned Parenthood of Southeastern PA v. Casey, 505 US 833. 1992. https://supreme.justia.com/cases/federal/us/505/833.

Popinchalk, Anna, and Gilda Sedgh. 2019. "Trends in the Method and Gestational Age of Abortion in High-Income Countries." *BMJ Sexual & Reproductive Health* 45(2): 95–103.

Prager, Joshua. 2013. "The Accidental Activist." *Vanity Fair* (January 18). www.vanityfair.com/news/politics/2013/02/norma-mccorvey-roe-v-wade-abortion.

PRRI. 2023. "Abortion Attitudes in a Post-Roe World." Public Religion Research Institute (February 23). www.prri.org/research/abortion-attitudes-in-a-post-roe-world-findings-from-the-50-state-2022-american-values-atlas.

PRRI. 2024. "Abortion Views in All 50 States." Public Religion Research Institute (May 2). www.prri.org/wp-content/uploads/2024/04/PRRI-April-2024-abortion.pdf.

Quinnipiac. 2021. "Nearly 8 in 10 Texas Voters Support Legal Abortion in Cases of Rape or Incest, Quinnipiac University Poll Finds; 63% of Texans Say Suing Schools Over Mask Mandates Is a Bad Idea." (September 29). https://poll.qu.edu/poll-release?releaseid=3822.

Rankin, Sarah. 2023. "Virginia Democrats Sweep Legislative Elections after Campaigning on Abortion Rights." *AP News* (November 8). https://apnews.com/article/virginia-legislature-election-2023-79f9337731c25decc83b83eeb4d3e00e.

Reproductive Freedom for All. 2004. "History" Last Accessed March 29, 2024. https://reproductivefreedomforall.org/about/history/.

Republican Party Platform. 1976. The American Presidency Project. www.presidency.ucsb.edu/documents/republican-party-platform-1976.

Republican Party Platform. 1980. The American Presidency Project. www.presidency.ucsb.edu/documents/republican-party-platform-1980.

Republican Party Platform. 2016. The American Presidency Project. www.presidency.ucsb.edu/documents/2016-republican-party-platform.

Roe v. Wade, 410 US 113. 1973. https://supreme.justia.com/cases/federal/us/410/113/.

Romero, Laura. 2023. "Virginia's Legislative Races Could Change Abortion Policy and Offer 2024 Clues: What to Know." *ABC News* (November 6). https://abcnews.go.com/Politics/virginias-legislative-races-change-abortion-policy-offer-2024/story?id=104587439.

Romo, Vanessa. 2023. "A Year after Dobbs and the End of Roe v. Wade, There's Chaos and Confusion." *NPR* (June 24). www.npr.org/2023/06/24/1183639093/abortion-ban-dobbs-roe-v-wade-anniversary-confusion.

Rose, Melody. 2007. *Safe, Legal, and Unavailable? Abortion Politics in the United States.* New York: CQ Press.

Rosenberg, Gerald N. 2008. *The Hollow Hope: Can Courts Bring about Social Change?* Chicago, IL: University of Chicago Press.

Rubella. (2020, December). Centers for Disease Control. www.cdc.gov/rubella/index.html.

Rust v. Sullivan, 500 US 173. 1991. https://supreme.justia.com/cases/federal/us/500/173/.

Ryan, Timothy J., and J. Andrew Ehlinger. 2023. *Issue Publics: How Electoral Constituencies Hide in Plain Sight.* Cambridge: Cambridge University Press.

Saad, Lydia. 2008. "Abortion Issue Laying Low in 2008 Campaign." Gallup (May 22). https://news.gallup.com/poll/107458/abortion-issue-laying-low-2008-campaign.aspx.

S.636 – 103rd Congress (1993–1994): Freedom of Access to Clinic Entrances Act of 1994. *Congress.gov*, Library of Congress, 26 May 1994, www.congress.gov/bill/103rd-congress/senate-bill/636/all-actions.

Sanger-Katz, Margot, and Claire Cain Miller. 2004. "How Common Is Medication Abortion?" *The New York Times* (March 26). www.nytimes.com/2024/03/26/upshot/medication-abortion-pill-use.html.

Seifter, Miriam. 2021. "Countermajoritarian Legislatures." *Columbia Law Review* 12(6): 1733–1800.

Serjeant, Jill. 2020. "Plaintiff in Roe v. Wade U.S. Abortion Case Says She Was Paid to Switch Sides." *Reuters* (May 19). www.reuters.com/article/us-usa-abortion-jane-roe/plaintiff-in-roe-v-wade-u-s-abortion-case-says-she-was-paid-to-switch-sides-idUSKBN22V33D.

Sherman, Mark. 2023. "Supreme Court Allows Idaho to Enforce its Strict Abortion Ban, Even in Medical Emergencies." *Associated Press* (January 5). www.pbs.org/newshour/politics/the-supreme-court-allows-idaho-to-enforce-its-strict-abortion-ban-even-in-medical-emergencies.

Shimabukuro, Jon O. 2009. "Abortion Law Development: A Brief Overview." Congressional Research Service (January 15). www.everycrsreport.com/

files/20090115_95-724_b1df583846fa83ea9362d860a04acacd57d81c15.pdf.

Sides, John, Chris Tausanovitch, and Lynn Vavreck. 2022. *The Bitter End: The 2020 Presidential Campaign and the Challenge to American Democracy.* Princeton, NJ: Princeton University Press.

Smith, Tom W., and Jaesok Son. 2013. "General Social Survey Final Report 2012: Trends in Attitudes towards Abortion." NORC, University of Chicago. www.norc.org/content/dam/norcorg/pdfs/Trends%20in%20Attitudes%20About%20Abortion_Final.pdf.

Smyth, Julie Carr. 2022. "Explainer: Abortion Landscape under 'Heartbeat Bills.'" *Associated Press* (June 29). https://apnews.com/article/abortion-us-supreme-court-health-ohio-tennessee-0056dcfb4e5fe1590f07b5993c52078a.

Solinger, Rickie. 2019. *Pregnancy and Power: A History of Reproductive Politics in the United States (Revised Edition).* New York: NYU Press.

Solly, Meilan. 2022. "Who Was Norma McCorvey, the Woman Behind Roe v. Wade?" *Smithsonian Magazine* (June 24). www.smithsonianmag.com/smart-news/who-was-norma-mccorvey-the-woman-behind-roe-v-wade-180980311/.

Spruill, Marjorie J. 2017. *Divided We Stand: The Battle over Women's Rights and Family Values that Polarized American Politics.* New York: Bloomsbury.

Stevens, Harry, and Colby Itkowitz. 2022. "What More than 1,000 Political Ads Are Arguing Right Before the Midterms." *The Washington Post.* www.washingtonpost.com/politics/interactive/2022/political-ads/?itid=lk_inline_manual_5.

Svolik, Milan W. 2019. "Polarization versus Democracy." *Journal of Democracy* 30(19): 20–32.

Texas Penal Code. 2023. Title 3, Chapter 12, Subchapter A. https://statutes.capitol.texas.gov/Docs/PE/htm/PE.12.htm#:~:text=FIRST%20DEGREE%20FELONY%20PUNISHMENT.

Theriault, Sean M. 2008. *Party Polarization in Congress.* Cambridge: Cambridge University Press.

Valentino, Nicholas A., Ted Brader, Eric W. Groenendyk, Krysha Gregorowicz, and Vincent L. Hutchings. 2011. "Election Night's Alright for Fighting: The Role of Emotions in Political Participation." *The Journal of Politics* 73(1): 156–170.

VanSickle-Ward, Rachel, and Amanda Hollis-Brusky. 2013. "An (Un) Clear Conscience Clause: The Causes and Consequences of Statutory Ambiguity in State Contraceptive Mandates." *Journal of Health Politics, Policy and Law* 38(4): 683–708.

VanSickle-Ward, Rachel, and Kevin Wallsten. 2019. *The Politics of the Pill: Gender, Framing, and Policymaking in the Battle over Birth Control.* New York: Oxford University Press.

VanSickle-Ward, Rachel, Adrian Pontoja, Morrey Liedke, and Dana Nothagle. 2023. "Abortion, Attitudes and Appointments: How Gender and Reproductive Rights Shaped Views on Amy Coney Barrett and Voter Turnout in 2020." *Journal of Women, Politics & Policy* 44(1): 40–55.

Walker, Amy Schoenfeld. 2023. "Most Abortion Bans Included Exceptions. In Practice, Few are Guaranteed." *The New York Times* (January 21). www.nytimes.com/interactive/2023/01/21/us/abortion-ban-exceptions.html.

Weber, Christopher. 2013. "Emotions, Campaigns, and Political Participation." *Political Research Quarterly* 66(2): 414–428.

Webster v. Reproductive Health Services, 492 US 490. 1989. https://supreme.justia.com/cases/federal/us/492/490/.

West, Darrell M. 2017. *Air Wars: Television Advertising and Social Media in Election Campaigns, 1952–2016.* Thousand Oaks, CA: CQ Press

Wilson, Joshua C. 2013. *The Street Politics of Abortion: Speech, Violence, and America's Culture Wars.* Stanford, CA: Stanford University Press.

Wolbrecht, Christina. 2000. *The Politics of Women's Rights: Parties, Positions, and Change.* Princeton, NJ: Princeton University Press.

Zaller, John. 1992. *The Nature and Origins of Mass Opinion.* Cambridge: Cambridge University Press.

Zernike, Kate. 2024a. "Texas Supreme Court Rejects Challenge on Exceptions to Abortion Ban." *The New York Times* (May 31). www.nytimes.com/2024/05/31/us/texas-abortion-ban-supreme-court.html.

Zernike, Kate. 2024b. "The Unlikely Women Fighting for Abortion Rights." *The New York Times* (May 27). www.nytimes.com/2024/05/27/us/abortion-women-tfmr.html.

Ziegler, Mary. 2020. *Abortion and the Law in America: Roe v. Wade to the Present.* Cambridge: Cambridge University Press.

Acknowledgments

The authors would like to thank Nichole Bauer, Rosalyn Cooperman, Jill Greenlee, Jenny Lobasz, Heather Silber-Mohamed, Montica Talmadge, Rachel VanSickle Ward, and Josh Zingher for their feedback. Thanks also to the participants at the 2023 meeting of the Empirical Study of Gender Research Network at Cornell University and attendees of the Emory Department of Quantitative Theory & Methods speaker series. This research was partially supported by a grant from the Center for American Women and Politics at Rutgers University and the Office of Student Research at Appalachian State University. We also thank our research assistants Spencer Whyte, Ted Wenner, Emma Shelby, Kathryn Hall, and Liza Constable for their work coding open-ended survey responses. Supplemental materials are provided in an online appendix.

Cambridge Elements

Gender and Politics

Tiffany D. Barnes
University of Texas at Austin

Tiffany D. Barnes is Professor of Government at University of Texas at Austin. She is the author of *Women, Politics, and Power: A Global Perspective* (Rowman & Littlefield, 2007) and, award-winning, *Gendering Legislative Behavior* (Cambridge University Press, 2016). Her research has been funded by the National Science Foundation (NSF) and recognized with numerous awards. Barnes is the former president of the Midwest Women's Caucus and founder and director of the Empirical Study of Gender (EGEN) network.

Diana Z. O'Brien
Washington University in St. Louis

Diana Z. O'Brien is the Bela Kornitzer Distinguished Professor of Political Science at Washington University in St. Louis. She specializes in the causes and consequences of women's political representation. Her award-winning research has been supported by the NSF and published in leading political science journals. O'Brien has also served as a Fulbright Visiting Professor, an associate editor at *Politics & Gender*, the president of the Midwest Women's Caucus, and a founding member of the EGEN network.

About the Series

From campaigns and elections to policymaking and political conflict, gender pervades every facet of politics. Elements in Gender and Politics features carefully theorized, empirically rigorous scholarship on gender and politics. The Elements both offer new perspectives on foundational questions in the field and identify and address emerging research areas.

Cambridge Elements

Gender and Politics

Elements in the Series

In Love and at War: Marriage in Non-State Armed Groups
Hilary Matfess

Counter-Stereotypes and Attitudes Toward Gender and LGBTQ Equality
Jae-Hee Jung and Margit Tavits

The Politics of Bathroom Access and Exclusion in the United States
Sara Chatfield

Women, Gender, and Rebel Governance during Civil Wars
Meredith Maloof Loken

Abortion Attitudes and Polarization in the American Electorate
Erin C. Cassese, Heather L. Ondercin and Jordan Randall

A full series listing is available at: www.cambridge.org/EGAP